PROBLEM SOLVERS

LUKE ZEDWICK

Cover Design by the Kuhn Design Group

ISBN: 978-1-7037-5365-3 (paperback/print)

CONTENTS

Foreword 5

Introduction 7

1. Learning from Teachers 15

2. Warm and Firm 25

3. Make a Plan 37

4. Attention Seeking 47

5. Birth of a Power-Struggler 61

6. Power-Struggling Mentality 77

7. See Your Ideal 89

8. Build a Ladder: Genuine Affection 97

9. Strategic Support 109

10. High Expectations 125

11. Grow Up with Them 139

12. Aim Small, Hit Small 151

About the Author 163

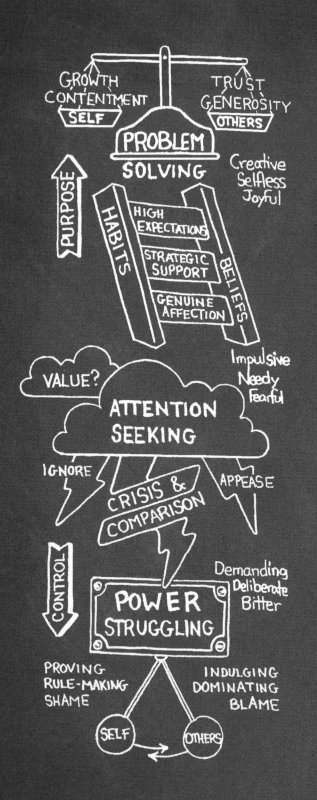

FOREWORD

By Dr. Corey Gilbert

Who do you listen to regarding parenting and skills to raise your children? Is it those you serve with intentionality and purpose? If you were to piece together the expertise and talent and training of an ideal leader for parents, I cannot imagine a better example and thought leader than Luke Zedwick. Luke is a father, a church leader, and a veteran in the public school system as a teacher and an administrator.

The way Luke thinks and has built a process that you and I can grab on to quickly, understand, and implement is a powerful gift. His ability to explain and empower you to careful thoughtful action can be life-altering in your skills and intentionality with your children. Many of Luke's approaches and concepts are counter-intuitive. Lean into them and even embrace them. I promise they will change your life and ministry to your own children.

One of the most difficult journey's we have as parents is dealing with difficult children and/or difficult times our children are navigating. Lean into Luke's Ladder and see it's purpose and power. Know that we often misinterpret our children's intent. Be willing to be wrong, admit a mistake and be an example.

Community is a key as well. Luke Zedwick has pieced together a powerful set of tools here, but they require the use of our community – those we have around us that we are doing life with. Expect more of your children. Raise the bar so that they have the honor of rising above each year of their life. Grow up WITH THEM.

I thank Luke Zedwick for his expertise and vulnerability in these pages. I hope you are challenged and your family tree is altered for the better after applying these tools and techniques. You will not regret it.

Dr. Corey Gilbert
HealingLives.com

INTRODUCTION

grew up knowing I wanted to be a teacher. I studied math and taught middle and high school for 11 years before somehow becoming an elementary principal in a town of 900 people. As a principal, I had big plans about how I would have a good, fatherly talk with the misbehaving kids, and how they would come to respect and look up to me. Boy was I wrong.

The kids, the parents, and my patient staff taught me over the next eight years that there is no simple or easy solution to changing kids' attitude or behavior. It takes months and years of patient determination and positivity. It's possible to train these kids to be comfortable in their own skin, to stop chasing the attention of their peers or adults, and instead, to make plans for their future that last longer than 30 seconds. But first, you have to do all those things for yourself. It's time to stop struggling as a mom or a dad and start building your own capacity to plan and execute as a parent. You can do it. I'll show you how.

I believe that in the heart of every person, young and old, is a question that must be dealt with first. If left unresolved, this question will haunt and poison the work you do and the relationships you try to maintain for your whole life. It will leave you alone and without purpose no matter what work you do or how many loving relationships you have. To the degree that you haven't dealt with this question will also affect how much satisfaction you're missing out on. The question is, do you matter?

I say "deal with," rather than "answer," because this question is a bottomless pit. The question of value is never really answered for anyone. It only works to sabotage what could replace it: the meaningful work you do and the cherished relationships you maintain. You know it's true because those two things, failure and rejection, are everyone's most common fear.

The people who lean on their egos end up on a quest for comfort, recognition, and ambition. They are plagued by ever increasing self-focus. Some become narcissistically obsessed with their image and the affirmation that social media is designed to feed them. Others become shame focused, making rules for themselves and fixated on the dream of being perfect as a mom, a wife, a professional, in their fitness, their spirituality, or their diet. There are endless ways to feed the question, but only one way to be free: walk away from it.

It's not a one-time decision, either. When we seek meaningful purpose that builds rich and lasting satisfaction, we can easily go astray as we try to control ourselves and others in order to avoid disaster. The fears creep back in. If you can control the people you love and the work you do, then perhaps you can be free from the fear. What you can't do is defeat fear by avoiding it. You can't avoid failure by not trying, or relationships by never being vulnerable. You can only overcome fear by going head on into it. Otherwise, it will poison the things you do and the love you share.

So the question of value, and our fear of failure and rejection, are always there. They haunt us as we watch our kids misbehave and our tempers flare. And that's why it sometimes seems as if every other article on parenting is how to stop feeling so bad about how you compare to other moms. The sad truth is that this question is a bottomless pit, and the more you try to control it, the more you try to answer it, the more hold it has upon you. Your only hope is to put it down and walk away. Stop trying to be a good parent. Stop trying to prove to yourself or anyone else (your kids included) that you have what it takes. Put the question down and walk away.

If you put down your question of value, even if just for a minute, then the frustration about being okay as a mother, or man enough to be a decent father, will be put down too. The farther away from it you get, the less personally you'll take it when your kids talk back or demand their way. Their public meltdowns and selfish demands won't be about you and your ego, they will be signs that your children are missing some skills to handle life's difficulties. Not only will you feel better as a parent when you stop trying to prove yourself, your kids will feel better too.

The purpose of this book is to look at the problems your kids face in not being able to concentrate on anything but video games, not being able to control their emotions when they face disappointment, failing to keep friends or understand social cues. Their own question of value is pouring fuel on the fire. Their insecurities don't come from a lack of self-esteem (trying to answer the question of value). They come from the same nagging fear that you face. They have to learn, just like you, to put it down and walk away. It's no easy task for a kid, but you can give them strength as you go through the process with them.

When our children fail to reach their potential, it's so often because they want to do things their own way. As parents, we can fall into the same trap. But there's a way to avoid it, the way of ancient wisdom and lived experience. When I was a classroom teacher, I wanted to find a way to bring the truths of the world to my students. I started teaching in a Christian school, but I knew that the truth was bigger than the experiences of youth groups and Sunday morning church. The capital "T" Truth is as vast as the universe. It crosses cultures and time periods, and it reaches into our hearts if we let it. So I began looking for wisdom from around the world. Wisdom for teenagers in need of it. I called it the Proverb of the Week.

Over the course of 19 years in education, as a middle and high school teacher, and then as an elementary school principal, these proverbs have grown into an entire curriculum of social skills and problem solving. At one point, I worked with a handful of teachers and administrators to develop lessons for the whole year. Later we added the 7 Habits of Happy Kids (inspired by the book of the same title by Sean and

Stephen R. Covey). Many people have helped to form it, and through the years this curriculum has morphed and changed. The one thing that remains is that we can draw from the wisdom of our ancestors to see the way we should go.

Though this book isn't Christian in nature, I am convinced that there is much wisdom to be gained from the Bible. Much of what I have learned about raising children, and how we often fail, is reflected in the ancient texts. I won't be citing scripture in order to convince you of things, but I believe that the Truth lives within those stories, and when we see them rightly, we will also see ourselves rightly. Our relationship with the endless perfection that we cannot reach (being the perfect parent, for example), will either set us on the path to growth and contentment, or it will send us into a spiral of comparing and controlling ourselves and others. Religion done rightly will always send us away from shame and blame and toward creative, selfless purpose. But it can be done wrong, as I'm sure you know.

One recurring theme of religions throughout the world is sacrifice. We sacrifice a sheep to the hungry wolf so it will not take our children. We sacrifice a bull to a perfect God because we have failed to live up to his standards and he may grow angry. But recently, I've been exploring a fascinating third perspective on this: the idea of sacrificing to a better future. Let me explain…

You may have heard of the oft-cited experiment where young children were given a marshmallow and asked to wait before eating it. If they could wait for a few minutes, they were told, they would get a second marshmallow. Those who waited longest as kids were far more likely to do well in their education, career, and marriage when tracked for the decades that followed. A sacrifice now could get you something better in the future.

If waiting a few minutes for sweets gets you a second marshmallow, then how much would waiting for a whole day get you? If waiting for a year is better still, how long could you postpone your gratification for even more rewards? Perhaps some of us could even invest in the next generation, so the world will be better for decades to come. The highest ideal, the most successful perspective would be to invest in eternity, and now you have religion. In this way, sacrifice isn't just the giving of money and time to avoid death or judgment from an impersonal diety. Your sacrifice is an investment into a future so distant that it may not appear in your lifetime: it is a treasure stored up in heaven.

Perhaps your relationship with your children is the opposite of investment: reaction and impulse. Perhaps it is based on fear. We might tell our spouse in the quiet moments, "If they keep this up, they won't have any friends. They won't find a career." And when you're being honest, you also admit that you've overused punishment or shame to try to influence your children. This is short-term thinking. You won't get any marshmellows.

Kids need to be trained, not punished, out of the bad habits that plague them, and the immediate feedback that punishment can provide should always be in the context of a larger story. That story is created by you, when you look at where they are now in their habits and beliefs, where you hope they'll be when they're 25 years old, and what it will take to get there. Don't just begin with the end in mind, connect the dots for them to overcome their faults and disadvantages.

I know there are many times that I have chosen to power struggle with my own kids, without thinking of their future, their story. As my boys grow older, though, I have been reminded again and again how much I have to let go of that crutch and bring the future into the conversation. It takes more effort, and the rewards come more slowly, but that's how all investments work. How am I training them to invest in themselves, their future families, their community, and beyond? Have I focused on fears of failure and instilled that in them? What will I do differently? How far into the future will I look, and how will I teach them to do the same?

Perhaps you've found yourself asking if parenting supposed to be this hard? Why do your kids get on your nerves so much, and what if you don't really like them right now? Does that mean you're failing? You've tried to do better, you've tried staying calm. Can it get better, because I know it can get worse? As someone who's worked with kids for more than two decades, from two-year-olds to 22, I can tell you that it can get better.

Fundamentally, the better way is the way of growth for yourself. The reason you're struggling to be a better parent is that you're also struggling to be a better person. You're struggling for control of yourself, to feel more successful as a parent, and wishing your kids would control themselves so you don't have to. Every once in a while, you'll get a glimpse of your sweet child: the one you know is in there, but as soon as something goes wrong, as soon as you expect them to behave like a normal human being, the drama and the struggle come roaring back. I hope this book can help.

CHAPTER 1

LEARNING FROM TEACHERS

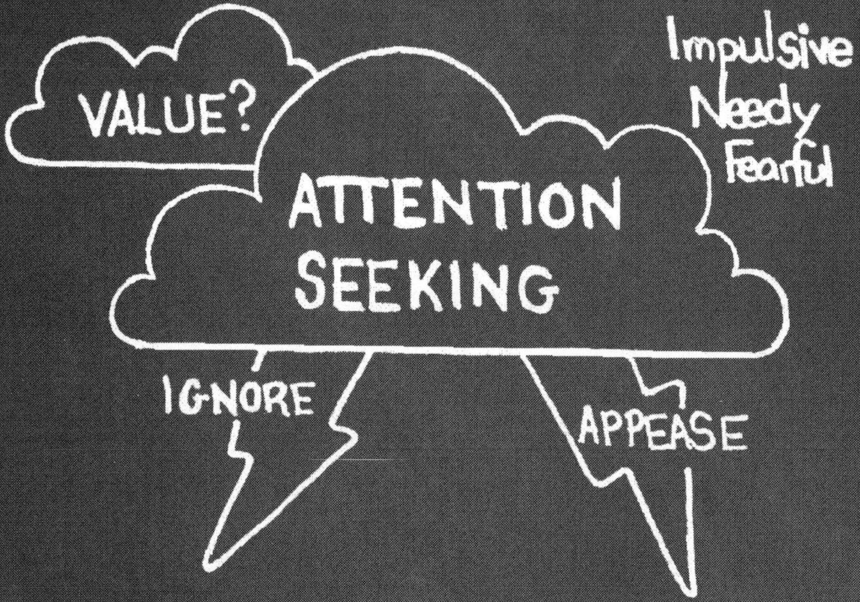
VALUE?
ATTENTION SEEKING
Impulsive
Needy
Fearful
IGNORE
APPEASE

As a classroom teacher for eleven years and a principal for eight, I have attended many trainings on how to improve my understanding and skills as an educator. Each new seminar is full of special jargon that claims to reinvent the traditional classroom and reach the unreachable child. I have tried not to fall for these sales pitches, which were almost always created by a researcher who had spent approximately five minutes in the last decade as an actual teacher. My goal was twofold: to better understand the process of teaching and learning, and to build a set of tools that would make me more effective.

Most of my efforts to improve were focused on something practical I could add that would fit with how I already did things. I was trying to add to my system, rather than reinvent it. I found these trainings followed a pattern: you walked out with 25 specific strategies that sounded good. You go back to your class and try five of them. Within a month, you were left with maybe one thing you had actually changed about your teaching. The only way to make a more significant change was for the whole teaching team to set out together to adopt a comprehensive strategy. One-time training or reading a book would never get me there, and no matter how good my intentions were, I would always fall back into my default way of teaching eventually.

For me, my fallback style of teaching was modeled after what I had seen from one of my favorite teachers as a kid. His name was Mr. Henderer, and he taught me seventh and eighth grade math. If there is an old-fashioned way to teach, he lived it out. He wore a short sleeved, white dress shirt every day, with a pocket protector full of pens. His glasses and slicked back hair made him look like he had just stepped out of the NASA control room for the moon landing. He had his routines and they rarely if ever changed. He was kind and patient, but he loved to teach math so that's what he did. There wasn't fluff or games, but for a kid like me it was just what I needed. That classroom became the default in my brain that was hard to change.

When I became an elementary school principal, I had to look at teaching in a whole new way. I had been a high school and middle school math and science teacher, but now I was coaching and supporting teachers in completely different circumstances, who were teaching things I never had. These teachers brought a wide variety of skill levels, and all of them had personalities and preferences I had not considered.

As I started, I found fads and old things reinvented. I heard complaints from veteran teachers about having seen it all before, and excited young teachers talking in fancy jargon. I soon learned that there were great teachers, people doing honest work, and then there were people who talked about other's weaknesses but couldn't face their own. Some teachers thought of themselves as the exception to every rule and loved to talk about their unique style, others made every thing a routine. What I was looking for is something timeless.

I say all this because teachers are just parenting a bunch of kids at once. All the lessons a teacher needs will apply to you as you raise your kids. You need to do it on purpose, with a goal for each lesson. Parenting has fads and jargon, and people who talk about their unique style but aren't willing to do the difficult work it takes to improve. There are researchers with little real experience and people selling 25 techniques that will eventually fade into some version of what your parents did, even though you grew up seeing all the weaknesses of their approach.

Some strategies for instruction just work, timeless ways of teaching and learning. In the same way, there are universal truths in parenting that I have seen while working with literally thousands of kids aged 5 to

25. For all their complexity and unique qualities, people aren't all that different from each other. Just like every person needs food, water, and air to breathe, every child needs love, support, and authority.

As a principal, disciplining kids is a big part of what I do. Every day I am faced with the hardest cases. They are the ones who get sent to the office, after all. Over the course of years, I learned that there are things you can do in the moment, and there are things that take years to sink in. I landed on a set of prioritized skills that every teacher needs, at every level, in order to be successful. I don't just mean for managing behavior, but to teach at the highest level. If I had a teacher struggling with clearly explaining things, for example, they had to get that figured out before I could begin supporting them in techniques for helping a few low performers, or to create high-level discussions and debate.

Parents get caught in the misconception that parenting isn't teaching, it's just getting kids to behave and survive childhood without anything terrible happening. They think that teachers have to prepare kids for intellectual tasks, whereas parents teach manners and self-control. I completely disagree. Is your vision of your child's future that they will be well-mannered but unable to think or stand up for what's right? Of course not.

You need to be developing supports for where your child is failing and engaging them in the high-level discussions and debates that will prepare them to think for themselves. If you leave these tasks to the teachers, you also leave them vulnerable to whatever political, spiritual, or philosophical beliefs those teachers might hold about the world. Having worked with many public-school educators, I can assure you there are many I wouldn't want indoctrinating my sons. Teaching is parenting and vice versa. That's not to say that teachers are better parents than everyone else, but the best teachers are also fantastic parents.

The goal of both is to not be needed anymore. That means your children are ready for what life will bring them, and it's a slow process. I see parents stuck in the same skill set they were using on toddlers, but they've got 10-year-olds who are thirsty for a wider view of the world. Honestly, I worry about the many adults I see who are way behind on that curve. They're not letting their kids have adventures (i.e., face real struggle) or solve problems. Then they wonder why those kids only want to stare at screens where heroes are having adventures and solving problems.

The fact is, if your child is six then you have 10 years of significant influence left. Where will you be in five years? In two? How ready will they be to face middle school peer pressure, or navigate the dark corners of the internet? You can't just teach them manners and make them clean their room when there are dragons to be faced. They need to train, and so do you. If we don't have a plan for our kids to level up, they will be learning these critical lessons the hard way. In order to make this plan, you're going to need to level up too.

DON'T POWER STRUGGLE

What parents and teachers often get stuck in, and we need a daily reminder at times, is the power struggle. As kids begin to feel the pull of a bigger, more significant world, they struggle for freedoms that they're not ready for. As a kid approaching middle school (and perhaps you remember this yourself), the constant comparison to others is intense. Other kids have the technology, fashion, and freedoms that you wish you had. Their families seem to have all the advantages, while your parents are strict and demanding or uninvolved and dysfunctional. The important thing to remember as the parent of such a kid is to not get caught in the struggle for power. You're the parent, you have the power, don't debate it.

One indicator that you're falling into a power struggle with your kids is how much you yell at them. You're yelling because they don't listen, but you're also teaching them that they don't need to listen until adults yell. I can tell you from experience that those kids struggle in school. Their teachers aren't yelling at them (hopefully), so kids draw two conclusions: I don't really have to do what they say because they're not mad yet, and teachers don't really care about me because people who care about me yell to keep me in line. It's time to calm down.

Your yelling is also a sign that you don't really believe you're in charge. You're using your power instead of your authority. There's an important difference. Your power comes from being bigger, better at arguing, and paying the bills. Authority, however, comes from your position as the parent, your love and sacrifice on their behalf, and the rightness of your point of view. You shouldn't be using power as the reason for their obedience. It teaches them Might Makes Right and that the bigger person is the one to be obeyed. It's subtle, but it creates kids whose goal is domination, and it pushes them toward more power struggling. Yelling really is a form of domination, after all.

Suppose you have to tell them three times to clean the kitchen, and on the third time you yell and threaten punishment. You tell yourself that they never listen until you yell. But that's not what they heard. What they heard you tell them is they should ignore you twice because you didn't really mean it, that they don't have to obey until people are mad, and that fear is the reason to do what's right. They're not practicing the mental discipline of deciding to do something they don't want to do so they can get a better outcome in the future. As a parent, you are eating your marshmallow rather than investing in the future (see introduction).

What if you made sure they heard you (because they're often not listening), told them once, and then calmly waited for them to comply. Don't walk away, don't yell. Then, inflict punishment only in the face of defiance. You'll get the "No Fair!" objection the first few times, but then they will learn that you mean it. You'll be using discipline and strength, rather than power and anger. You'll be training them to stop what they want to do so they can do what's right. And because you're there with them, they'll see you investing in their obedience, helping them avoid failure, and keeping high expectations because you believe in their potential. They won't really notice all that, but that's the long-term lesson.

I think we would do well to bring back rightness as a sufficient reason for things. Kids are wonderful and innocent, but they're also foolish and inexperienced. Being a kid is reason enough for them to not get their way, but you don't need to tell them that. You do need to know it yourself. Your position as parent can give you confidence in your parenting. Confidence combined with genuine patience is enough to stop the power struggle from your side, and your side is enough because there are no one-sided power struggles. Don't force your will on them, bring them under your authority with patience and respect. They deserve respect because they matter, not because they're right or powerful. Hear them out, tell your side, then make your decision and enforce it.

Part of the reason your kids may not be as emotionally strong as they should be is that we've been keeping them from the risks of failure and rejection that they absolutely need to face. We follow them around and keep them from getting hurt, we make sure no one is mean to them, we don't let them know that they lost the game, or they didn't make the grade. We put pads on their elbows and knees and hope they won't have low self-esteem. When we do this, we're making our decisions based on fear.

If, however, we let them fail and fight and learn things the hard way at a young age, then they will be far more able to handle the failures and rejection that come when they're older. That doesn't mean you create the descent into chaos that happened in *The Lord of the Flies* in your house or neighborhood. It does mean that you give them room to work it out with help when they need it. Hopefully, they'll be more centered in themselves when they enter middle and high school. Centered, after all, simply means that they're less prone to fear-based decision making.

Facing fear at an early age makes kids less likely to go chasing ego-builders that destroy relationships and create unhealthy comfort seeking such as alcohol, drugs, gambling, sex, etc. They pursue these things in part because they numb the endless comparisons that the fear creates. Comparison starts to haunt them in early adolescence and is the spark of many an argument between children and parents. If your goal as a parent is to work yourself out of a job, meaning they're ready for what life brings, then your kids have to work through failure and rejection. If you are helping them avoid those lessons out of your own fear, you only push the lesson farther into the future. When the inevitable lessons come, they will be learned the hard way, when the stakes are much higher.

RESTRAINT TRAINING

At school, there are lots of rules and limits about when you can put your hands on an out-of-control kid to stop them or move them. It's called restraint training, and you practice how to get out of being bitten, having your hair pulled, being kicked and attacked. I have experienced all these things, and I can tell you it is very hard in that moment not to get frustrated.

Q-TIP was the acronym we learned: quit taking it personally. Their anger isn't about you. Their bad behavior, even their anger at you, really isn't about you. They are expressing the chaos they feel and the skills they're missing. Your job is to help them get through it now and learn how to deal with the next wave of fear and fury that will always come. As the adult, you can't let your anger get the better of you, even when a kid who is doing everything they can to hurt you. It makes the situation exponentially worse.

It's sad to think about what a kid has to go through that they would be willing to kick a window with a running start or hit their own head against the concrete sidewalk. Willing isn't quite the word, though, because at some point they are genuinely out of control. Their rage and pain have taken over. They are willing to do anything to control you, to feel safe, including hurt themselves. Kids don't get to that state in a day, and they don't come out of it quickly either.

Disability can play a large part in how some kids handle stress, and there's sometimes nothing you can do to change how their brains are wired. Even those kids can learn to cope and predict their outbursts over time. But most violent kids I've worked with are survivors of trauma or abuse. They aren't born into struggle and fighting and outburst and rage, they are trained by the intent of the adults in their lives or the circumstances outside their control. As heartbreaking as that is, it also means that they can be trained to think in a new way. It takes years of patient intervention and parental support, but I've seen it work.

Hopefully, you'll never have to go through that with your own kids, but it doesn't have to get to that level for it to be a genuine power struggle. Chances are good that your kids have their tantrums and such, but the fact that you're reading a book on how to be a good parent means you're invested. That's a good start. What you also need is support for how to give your kids the skills to handle the trauma they will experience, even if it's a milder form. The support you offer and the strength you show in holding your kids to a high standard will go far in avoiding the power struggles you'll face as a parent.

CHAPTER 2

WARM AND FIRM

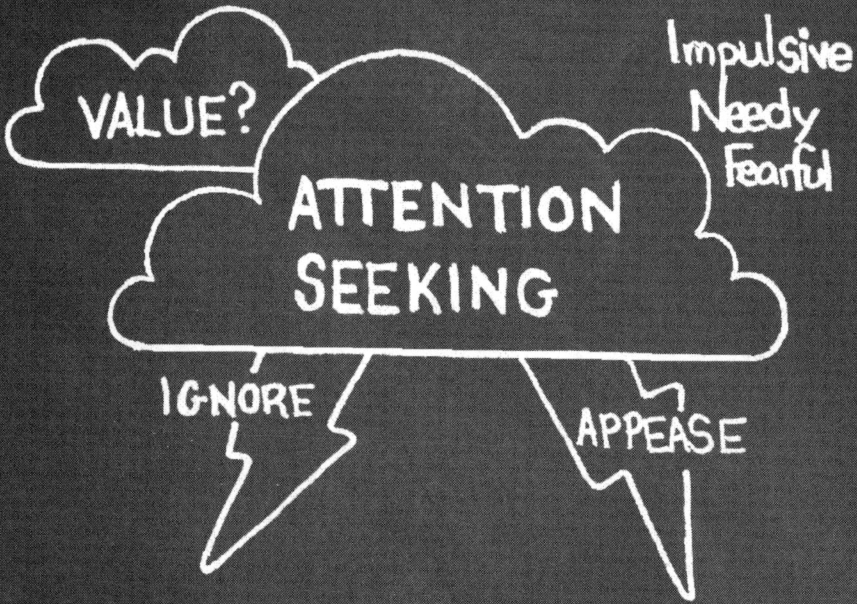
VALUE?
ATTENTION
SEEKING
Impulsive
Needy
Fearful
IGNORE
APPEASE

n the classic book *Teach Like a Champion*, there's a section on how to manage misbehavior. One strategy is called Warm and Firm. That section talks about a misconception some teachers have that being firm means you can't be warm. I love that language and use it often. Some parents think of themselves as the warm and affectionate one, but they wonder why kids eventually push back against them and reject that affection. Others think they're the demanding type, and they find kids resenting them and looking for underhanded ways to defy their authority. Both types think it's either one or the other, but the best parents are both warm and firm. It's what kids want and need.

When you're not firm as a parent, kids simply stop trusting you or respecting your opinion. You don't mean what you say, and they know it. If you're not able to stand up against them, then how will you protect them from other kids? If their whining and back talk cause you to give in, if your will is that weak, then you're not strong enough to keep them safe from the meaner kids. You may love them, but what are you going to do when the meaner and bigger people come to hurt them? You will give in to those people too. You might get angry at their teacher and talk about how you're the mama bear that shouldn't be messed with, but it's not a long-term investment and they know it.

When you let them manipulate you with bad behavior, you also are letting them fail repeatedly. Disobedience and the chaos it creates is failure. They may like getting their way, but they hate that they're failing. Haven't you ever enjoyed indulging in bad behavior but resented yourself and others later on? It is demoralizing in the long term. You're leaving them to fend for themselves, but they don't have the skills or self-control to do it well. The desire to be the warm and caring parent can lead you down a lonely road where kids lose any respect for you protecting or guiding them.

On the other side of that error is the parent whose firm demeanor is destroying their relationships with their children. They withhold time and connection because kids have to "earn it". They say things like, "They just want attention, so I'm not going to give it to them." When their kids misbehave, they're excluded from fun times (which is a great discipline strategy) and sent away from the adults for extended periods (not so good). This works if the parent has followed up within a few minutes, but to exclude a kid for long can be a trap. Worse still is the parent who disciplines in public. It may be out of frustration, as an expression of a twisted desire to humiliate, or probably a bit of both. These overly firm parenting methods create in your child a simmering desire for vengeance, an undercurrent of self-hatred, and a need to control.

I once had a very wise school principal who mentored me in leadership and school discipline. She would tell parents whose child was in trouble, "Whether your child is in trouble or rewarded, they should be with you." They can do fun things with you, or they can do chores in silence. With you. Keep them close so they know they matter, even when they fail.

AVOIDING FAILURE

Annie Duke, a professional poker player and author of the book *Thinking in Bets: Making Smarter Decisions When You Don't Have All the Facts*, teaches about risk. In it, she describes Seattle Seahawks coach Pete Carroll, who called a controversial play in the closing seconds of Super Bowl XLIX. He's faced with four possibilities:

1. If he calls the play that everyone expects, and it works, then he will be rewarded with praise.

2. If what's expected fails, then it will be just bad luck.

3. If he makes an unorthodox decision and wins, he will be lauded as a brilliant strategist.

4. But (and this is the question of greatness), if the risky, possibly better move doesn't work out, then everyone and their cousin will come down on that failure as the single biggest mistake possible.

And that's what happened. With short time and few yards to score, he called a pass play instead of the expected run up the middle. Go watch the last seconds of the 2015 super bowl and interception that ended the game. See the criticism Carroll got for that call. The insults and outbursts lasted weeks, and the fact that he had strong reasons for the call didn't matter. When the unorthodox move fails, everyone jumps on the bandwagon of criticism.

Parents too have no shortage of criticism for one another. When parents or teachers get it wrong, they're usually making the same mistake: they're avoiding the conflict and the failure and vulnerability that is required to get through it together. Self-protection is a relevant concern, and you do have to choose your battles on a daily basis, but exceptions don't make the rule. Your best moments as a parent are when it's not about your ego. Take yourself out of the equation and go through the conflict for the sake of your child. There will come a time in your life as a parent where you will have to decide whether to keep doing the thing you've always done, which kind of works and everyone expects you to do, or risk failure in order to reach for something better. Will you do the good work that might not work out? Or will you protect your ego?

Every year, someone seems to publish a survey of people's biggest fears. Always at the top of the list seems to be public speaking. In one setting you have the potential loss of two of the most fundamental needs every person shares: to be useful and to be valued. Or to put it in reverse: rejection and failure. People have nightmares about getting to school without pants on, of being chased by wolves or having their teeth fall out. At the heart of every person are two questions: *Am I valuable?* and *Am I making a difference?* Like public speaking, parenting wraps up both those questions and pounds you with them day after day.

The biggest fear we face as parents is whether we've failed our kids in raising them. If our kids misbehave in public, what does that say about us and our value? The result of this thinking, once it takes hold, is that we very quickly begin disciplining our kids so we don't look bad. If we're not careful, we create a public and private persona, where our kids' misbehavior gets ignored until it embarrasses us. Then it gets met with threats and raised voices, but no real long-term intentions to train them in good behavior.

The most effective parents and teachers I've known see behavior management as a long-term culture building, not rule-setting and enforcement. Do's and Don'ts come from what's important to us, and they're easily explained and enforced as part of our community values we've established. Once kids are 8 or 9 years old, a system of discipline can start to be preemptively created based on what you care about, rather than just a series of reactions you have depending on their attitudes and actions. The latter is prone to depend on how hungry or tired you are as a parent, and then you'll end up disagreeing with your spouse when they're less or more exhausted. But you can set up a system of values and expectations ahead of time, and enforcing it won't depend on which kid is getting on your nerves.

For parents who choose fear as their guiding principle, the only thing worse than feeling like a failing parent is your child not loving you. For smaller kids, this can happen for any reason, and most often because you don't give them what they want. Your fear lets their emotions rule your home because you avoid enforcing your expectations for fear of a tantrum. You might tell them to stop, but you don't mean it. You walk away and say don't do it again, but they do. You can tell whether you've been raising your kids in fear by how well they've learned to threaten you with rejection. Maybe they do it to your spouse, their teachers, or anyone in authority. If I don't get my way, you will get my anger, hatred, isolation, or rejection. When kids see their emotions as a method of argument, you are training them to be manipulative in their most meaningful relationships. They become little narcissists because you didn't want to hurt their feelings. This is a recipe for disaster in their future relationships.

APPEASE AND CONTROL

Here's another ineffective method I've seen parents use to shelter their children from the pain and sadness that failure bring: appeasing them. We've all done it sometimes, but some people do it way too much: giving them what they demand, covering their mistakes, and cleaning up their messes. This is how you make tyrants, and it's often where their disrespect originates. When you appease dictators, they just hate you even more. You see, tyrants of all kinds (historical and familial) view appeasers as the weakest of all people. Let me say it again, when you appease your children's bad behavior, you're training them to be manipulative in their future relationships.

I believe this is partly why kids are more likely to disrespect their mothers than their fathers. They want the approval that's hardest to get, and the parent whose praise isn't connected to effort will see that praise devalued. Add to that the tendency of mothers to share their children's pain and therefore avoid conflict that causes it. When we appease the emotional outbursts, then we have a recipe for contempt. Even though your love isn't connected to performance, your praise and approval should be based on effort. In doing this, you put a premium on said praise. Over time, you will cultivate a healthy fear of disapproval and a craving for success. This success builds legitimate confidence in the long term because confidence comes from overcoming real obstacles. That's why participation trophies not only don't build self-esteem, but they actually thwart the real confidence that comes from facing failure and not giving up.

This kind of performance-based praise also creates real empathy in your kids. Research shows that just giving empathy to your children, while good for them in moderation, doesn't make them more empathic. If overdone, it actually makes them more narcissistic. When you over-value their hurt feelings, it makes them believe their emotions are paramount. Without the high expectations and real consequences (most often associated with fathers), kids aren't made to face the impact of their failure. "Look what you did" is a powerful statement from any source, and it causes kids to see what others are feeling. That's how empathy is made.

The reason your kids try out manipulation and disrespect—and all kids try this out at some stage—is because they've seen it work. Perhaps they saw a friend do it to their parents, or maybe a classmate tries it on the teachers at school. Fundamentally, if it becomes a pattern in your household, it's because you're losing the battle of wills that your kids need to lose. Part of loving means letting go of control, and when you can't do that, you're letting fear win. When you encounter this form of manipulation, you have to address it head-on.

Emotional manipulation is a poison to all forms of relational health, and it may be that you're the one teaching it. Are you using your position over your kids in a manipulative way? It's always a good idea to check how often you use your own anger or frustration to convince your kids to obey or do what's right. Maybe you don't say that, but is it what your kids take away from your discipline? To the degree that your kids get away with things based on which parent is home, whether it's the end of a hard week, etc., is the degree you're being manipulative with them. The only real reason for rules and consequences is that your kids need them. Don't think that you're not also putting up with this kind of behavior in your marriage. The values and boundaries you've set as a family will need to be fought for.

If you avoid the pitfall of limitless approval and the emotional tyranny of the needy child, then you may yet fall into the pit on the other side. Where one parent may want to appease and rescue, the other will often tend toward a mind-set of control. Controlling your child's every choice in order to keep them from ever failing is just as destructive as making a tyrant. While your kids are growing up in front of you, you're still thinking of them as helpless, not ready for the wide world.

You need a plan that prepares them for real risk, and that means giving them incrementally larger responsibilities.

Kids who are faced with controlling parents begin finding little rebellions wherever they can. They repress the behaviors that draw their parents' wrath but don't resolve the unmet needs that such behavior may be indicating. That's not to say that bad behavior always reflects some deep need. Sometimes kids are just selfish and naughty. But a child who doesn't grow up into a set of choices and consequences (i.e. responsibility) will crave it on an emotional level that they almost never understand consciously. Those kids' need for adventure, for personal expression, for a genuine purpose, will begin to warp their desires and surface later on with compulsive behaviors of all sorts.

To the degree that our aim is to avoid discomfort for those we love, including our children, our conversations become more and more shallow. This problem is rampant throughout our communities. "Polite people don't talk about religion and politics," we are told. But of course, religion and politics are just a reflection of our fundamental values and how we hope to improve the world around us. If we want to build our communities and create civility in disagreement, we have to practice. If we want to learn from each other and see the world more clearly, if we believe that the person who disagrees with us may have something to teach us, then we must engage in meaningful conversation. The same is true of our children, who also have something to teach us.

That's not to say that we should make a habit of spouting dogmatic statements that we heard from the internet and acting like we're being deep or intellectual. If we just repeat the beliefs approved by the leaders of whatever social group we've joined, then we aren't really thinking. The greatest risk of this kind of behavior is that we end up disagreeing with ourselves in the end. We will say we agree with one thing, but the deepest part of ourselves will fight against it with impulsive and embittered actions. We have to integrate the things we believe from a large scale (religious and political doctrines) with the real-life experiences and personality within each of us. Teach your children to do the same through meaningful conversation that includes disagreement. Don't get in the habit of appeasement or control.

TEACH THEM HOW TO FIGHT

To have those conversations, we need ground rules on how to fight. These ground rules can be a great boundary within marriage as well. The way we fight with our spouse will greatly affect how our kids see what's normal in their future relationships. There are a few research-supported boundaries that work not only in marriage but with every disagreement you encounter.

The first rule of healthy disagreement is no criticism. You don't get to speak to what someone always does, or how they failed you before and now they're doing it again. The person across from you is not the enemy, whether they're your spouse or your child. Nearly all conflict comes from unmet expectations, and that means you're expecting more of yourself or others than they're willing to give. Working out how you've disagreed with yourself or your family is no easy task, and personal attacks only make it worse. Don't criticize.

The next rule is to dive into the conflict with the aim of resolving it. No stonewalling, and definitely no agreeing to things you don't actually think are right. If you want to sabotage agreements and build up resentment toward the people you love, try saying it's fine when it's not, or that you will when you know you really won't. You may not want to argue, but lying to yourself and others about it doesn't work. Don't keep the peace by avoiding conflict, work for peace through real engagement with the matters at hand. This takes substantial strength of character, especially if you're avoiding the other pitfalls of arguments. There is immense wisdom in choosing your battles carefully, but you do need to figure out what you care about. What are the hard lines you need to draw for yourself? Work them out with the ones you love.

That's why family meals are so important. They are the best place to have these conversations. Whether you're at the holiday table or just an evening meal with your kids, the people you love are the ones you need to fight with the most. What you'll find over time is that you'll fight less and less. The big deals will be worked out, and the little things will bother you less and less. Fighting less is only a good indicator of relational health if you've fought through the things you needed to. Perhaps you need to fight. Perhaps there are issues that you have to work out with someone. The more the little things are bothering you, the more work there is to do on the fundamentals. Don't stonewall.

Rule number three is no defensiveness. In any argument, you will be faced with your own failures. Failures are hard to face, and people's most common response is to compare themselves with others so they can feel better. In a fight, this comes out as defensive attacks. There's no clearer sign of shame, and the tendency is always to turn attention away from our faults. But you can't grow that way, and the goal of any relationship is to create safety to fail. That's why the first rule is to not criticize. There's nothing wrong with sadness in the face of failure, but there's nothing fun about it either. When someone doesn't feel safe to fail, they will default to defensive attacks and blaming others. That sense of danger may be coming from their upbringing or from something you've done. Either way, let this be a hard boundary for your arguments with your kids or your spouse. Don't get defensive.

The last rule is that you do not show contempt. That means no eye rolling, no sighing with disgust, none of it. According to the research of John Gottman at the University of Washington, if you or your spouse tend to use any of these four behaviors in disagreement, the chance that you'll get divorced in the next decade is incredibly high. With disgust/contempt, the rate approaches 90%. This kind of behavior isn't just pointing out faults, but it speaks to the actual value of the other person. Showing disgust at the feelings or opinions of your spouse in front of your kids will also drive a wedge between you and them. If you need more convincing, think on this: psychologists have observed that disgust is the root emotion for racism and genocide in places where mass murder has actually taken place. It isn't hatred, and it isn't revenge. Your disgust at your spouse is the seed of murder. Root it out of your marriage and your family.

If making your spouse or kids feel worthless is okay with you—because that's what disgust does—then you need to ask yourself what has led you down this kind of road. What's the big deal you didn't resolve in the past that's made every little deal since then build up to the point that resentment takes over? Perhaps that's how you've always dealt with conflict. If so, then the probability is high that your bitterness (and that's what it is) isn't about your spouse or your kids at all. Someone before them is still pulling at your heart from the distant past and poisoning your relationships now. If left unresolved, the chances are high that you will be passing that same festering resentment to your children as well. It's time to face the past so that little deals can stay little. Don't show contempt.

The goal of all parenting is not to avoid conflict, failure, or suffering. These are the things of life. Our goal is to give our children the tools and the strength to navigate conflict, failure, and suffering in a way that not only gives them value and health, but gives it to the ones they love, the community in which they live, and all of them now and into the future. It's a tall order and fraught with risks on every side, but you can't avoid this conflict. Don't forget that the goal of every parent is to not be needed. This doesn't happen by accident.

CHAPTER 3

MAKE A PLAN

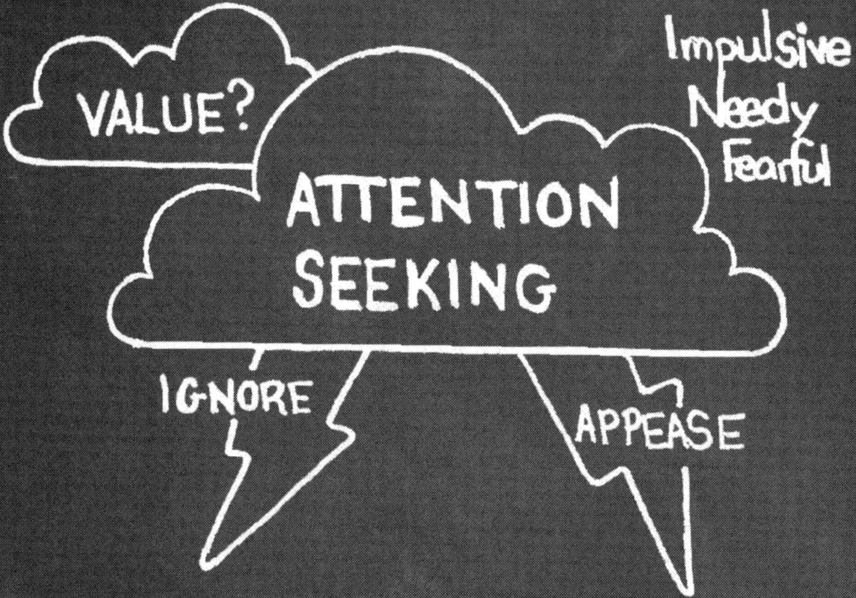
VALUE?
ATTENTION SEEKING
Impulsive
Needy
Fearful
IGNORE
APPEASE

One of the big symptoms of kids who've been starved for value is their thought process is consistently impulsive. They do things without thinking. You know these kids because when you ask them why they did something, they always shrug and give you that look of guilt and frustration. They really don't know why they did it. They were just hungry for something. But before I go into the practical support for kids' impulsive behavior, let me pause and address something more important.

As a parent, I want to give you some targets to aim for when your kids are like this, but don't forget that all kids face this sometimes. Your question of value as a mom or dad might be rearing up right now. You might be thinking of your own kid and calling yourself a failure because they get into the attention-seeking mind-set. Don't do it.

Remember that your own question of value is the first thing to block your ability to help your child deal with theirs. If you're going to create a home where kids are safe to struggle and grow, then you have to be safe too. Put down your question of value. That's the only way to be free from it. Walk away from trying to prove that you're a good parent (or a good wife, daughter, employee, etc.). Instead, it's time to stand firm upon the nobility of purpose that parenthood brings you. The work itself can be the emotional satisfaction you will live on. You're learning to put down your ego so you can help your kids deal with theirs. Now back to parenting.

Here's what you can start doing right now: teach them to stop and think. Planning ahead is a skill that most kids don't get quickly. You can teach them how to do it in four simple (but difficult) steps:

1. Verbalize your plans,

2. Ask them to verbalize their plans,

3. Let them try out their plans,

4. Reflect with them afterward.

Start explaining how you make decisions about time and money. Tell them stories about the mistakes you've made in the past. Be a teacher. The dinner table and car rides work great for this. Talk about pros and cons, and definitely talk about trade-offs. That was the biggest lesson I learned as a young principal: hard decisions are rarely about right and wrong. They almost always become a quest for the best choice among many, with losses and gains for each option. Your fundamental values have to be your guide in the final decision, so if you've never put them into words, now's the time to start. Doing that with your kids is a great idea, but a word of warning: once you say that family time is more important than screen time, for example, you better be prepared to live up to it. They are going to ask you why you're watching that program after they go to bed, or why you're on your phone when you said you couldn't jump on the trampoline because you needed to get work done. Respond humbly and openly. Verbalize your plans.

The subjects of time and money are a good place to start because those are very practical things they need to start working with at a young age. Whenever they come into money, start asking them what their plans are for it. Vague answers aren't good enough. They'll probably need reminding that they've been wanting the new game or shoes or sports ball, so help them make a plan to get it. Also, don't be satisfied with their cop-out that they don't want it anymore when they realize they'll have to work for it. Give that legitimacy, but then come back later and make the plan. What they mean when they say they don't want to work for it is that they don't have the discipline to save or work or plan for their future. If the marshmallow test was true of 5-year-olds, then it's true of teenagers. Discipline is taught by caring leaders, so be that for them. Ask them to verbalize their plans.

The next step is the hard one for many parents. Kids make plans that are often ridiculous, but they need to try them out. You're teaching them to plan, but you're also teaching them to learn from errors and improve their choices based on feedback. Remember, we're not ignoring or appeasing them, but we're supporting them in taking real risks. If their plans won't result in injury or arrest, try to say yes to them. Let them experiment and build and take risks. That's not the same as doing impulsive and stupid things. Those happen anyway, but the same behavior with a plan that was explained and justified will result in a lesson learned. Impulsive mistakes rarely result in growth, but a prediction of outcomes and consequences can go a long way. Let them try out their plans.

What you're trying to do is teach them to actually think. So don't just let them convince you with smooth sounding words. What you don't want is your 17-year-old coming home with some kind of catastrophe like a car accident or arrest and say that they just weren't thinking. Learning the hard way is not good when there's that much at stake, so you need to start early and often teaching them to reflect on their plans.

Don't be afraid to present to them the weaknesses in their plan and help them (not just make them) improve it. Ask questions and give input. "Here's where I'm worried it will fail. Have you thought of this?" "Here are the people you'll need to check with. How are we going to do that?" Once the plan is complete, check back in. Ask questions such as, "Was it harder or easier than you thought it would be? Did you get what you hoped for?" Reflect with them afterward.

A simple example of this was when our boys were younger and they wanted to mix things together into their clear plastic water bottles. They started with soap, and then table salt and orange juice. They called it their potion, and once they took it outside it included dirt and leaves and whatever they could find around the house. When I first saw them doing this, my impulse was to make my own prediction about it ending up as a mess in the kitchen, or that they would try to trick a younger brother into drinking it. But instead of putting my foot down, I came to them and presented my concerns. "I see what you're doing, I'm worried about these bad things happening, what is your plan?" They assured me they wouldn't trick anyone, that they would dispose of it properly afterward, and that there wouldn't be a hole in the lawn when they were done. Off they went feeling like they had convinced their dad of their plans. They did most of the things in their plan, but that game also became a staple in our household for over a year. I'm convinced they enjoyed the game more because they got to choose it and complete a plan with feedback and real accountability.

As they verbalize their plans, ask good questions of them. Genuinely let them plan, and don't try to take over. Watch out that they're not just telling you what you want to hear. The best opportunities come when they come to you with a request: "Can we go to the store?" "Can we ride our bikes around the neighborhood?" This is your chance to ask questions that show you take their ideas and desires seriously. Ask, "Who will be there?" "How long will it take?" "Will it be hard or easy and why?" That last question is a good one, because it can start a healthy thought pattern when anxiety and uncertainty start to grow in adolescence.

IGNORE AND EXPLODE

One big mistake I see some parents using to deal with their children's attention-seeking is to ignore them. "They just want attention, so don't give it to them" the thinking goes. The result is almost always disaster. Attention-seekers are so emotionally hungry, they are going to take their behavior to whatever level it takes to get your attention, and the more they're ignored the more starvation they'll feel. If that means infuriating you, then so be it. Even your negative attention proves their point: that you care about them. The worst treatment you can give them is the one that makes them hungrier, so don't starve them of the thing they're dying to get. If they were thirsty, you wouldn't say "They just want water, so don't give it to them." Feeling valuable works the same way.

What ends up happening is that you get into a cycle with your children of ignoring and exploding. Like a pendulum swinging back and forth. You try to stay calm, but their fearful neediness is draining, and you eventually start to resent them. They increase their misbehavior in response. They would rather you yell than say nothing, not just because they're angry or defiant, but because yelling is a form of paying attention. A parent who yells cares on some level. No one gets that upset about something they don't care about. But as a parent, your anger is selfish: you want them to stop bothering you far more than you want them to learn to relate to authority. It's not a strategy of support, it's a tantrum. They eventually learn that too, and now you're resenting each other. Soon you're feeling ashamed about disliking your child, but it only shortens your fuse. The pendulum swings higher. Perhaps you try to deny it, but a cycle of struggle is beginning to form in your relationship with your child.

You've experienced this effect when you've seen other parents, perhaps even friends or family members, being harsh with their own kids while you looked on with compassion for the child stuck in obvious fear and need. Have you noticed how easy it can be to validate someone else's child? But for your child, there's a long history. If you've been ignoring bad behavior and cries for attention, you will eventually dislike your children. If you struggle to like your kids, imagine how hard it will be for the other kids in their class, for their teachers even. Their fuses may be much shorter, and they'll struggle to connect with people everywhere they go.

I learned this lesson once when I collected a set of impulsive, attention-seeking boys from the fifth grade whose teachers were struggling to establish rules in their classes. Each Wednesday these boys would come to my office for lunch, and we'd talk about what it meant to grow up into young men. They had thoughtful things to share, many of their ideas were regurgitated from culture and family, but they were trying them on for size. That's a big part of adolescence. One boy said, when talking about his parents and teachers, "I don't even listen to adults until they yell at me. That's how I know they mean it." If he wasn't careful, he was on his way toward a cycle of struggle with all the adults in his life. They all were.

But one boy, let's call him Alex, simply couldn't stop interrupting, even in such a small group. He would blurt out noises, silly jokes, and purposefully annoying comments. When it became a pattern, we actually talked about his behavior right there in front of him. I told the kids that he was trying for attention so let's all just ignore him. Classic mistake. It only got worse. I tried having the whole group physically turn their bodies away from him each time he squawked, but he only saw that as making the game more fun. It was like trying to come up with a comeback to someone's insult only to find out that it feeds their game and makes them want to win. Then it dawned on me: he was hungry. Let's feed him.

We made a plan: from that point on whenever Alex would squawk or joke or disrupt an important moment in the conversation, all our eyes would calmly and kindly turned toward him. We agreed as a group that we wouldn't shame him or exclude him, but we'd give him what he was asking for. And it was amazing to watch as all that attention would be poured on him at once. He would sit with the biggest smile while we all looked straight at him. It only took a few seconds before he would relent in joyful embarrassment. After a half dozen tries at this, he started to interrupt less and less. We were building a culture of positive accountability.

Then something interesting happened. He started to disrupt not out of impulse, but deliberately. His comments became targeted and negative. He was shifting into something more severe, and I took more serious steps. I warned him that that wasn't okay and he would not be invited to lunches if he continued. It didn't stop, and I made good on my word. Even with all those other boys around, Alex cried when I told him he couldn't come back. He was facing his failure and its consequences. Within two weeks I approached him and invited him to come back into the group. He was a changed boy. He had struggled with impulse, then he struggled with resentment. Finally, he found acceptance.

If one parent is more likely to ignore a child, it's often been true in my experience that the other wants to appease them and rescue them out of the messes they've made. Appeasing parents are often convinced that their child is special in some way that means the normal rewards and consequences of life should not apply to them. Researchers are beginning to label these moms and dads as lawnmower parents.

Once we had helicopter moms who made sure that their kids got every advantage. Their goal was nothing scary: no gluten, no nuts, no sugar or food dye. Safety first. Then we got tiger moms who were building their child's resume before they even entered kindergarten. Today we have lawnmower parents who bring in the special water bottle to class that their child left in the car for the tenth time this month. They aren't even protecting their feelings or fearful of injury or failure. They're afraid of the emotional wrath of their child. They're so afraid of the rejection that their child might wield that they will mow over anything and anyone who might say no. All this fear made their kids more frail, expecting the whole world to protect them.

What the child eventually comes to understand is that the adult who is always protecting or removing obstacles is doing so because they don't believe in them. How many times have you said of your child (especially your youngest), that they just can't handle that yet? They're too little. How often are you shocked that anyone would expose your child to that kind of punishment or allow that kind of freedom to fail? Perhaps you've fallen into the trap of the lawnmower.

Appeasing parents are also the ones who are constantly telling their child they're so smart or so beautiful, as if those were the highest ideals one can attain. For the most part, kids can't change either one of those things no matter how hard they work. What experience and research have taught us is that these kids, even those who may be quite gifted, can also be the most emotionally fragile and likely to quit. The way you praise them makes all the difference because it tells them what's most important. Praise hard work and perseverance, and they'll put those values at the center. Recognize the things they can't change ("You're so talented"), and you tell them that the most important thing in life is the thing you can't change.

That can build up the ego of a kid who fares well in the comparison game, but it also makes them vigilant for anyone who might be better. Kids who actually believe you about their unrecognized genius or beauty, are the most distraught when any evidence arises that threatens that most prized label. Failure becomes the biggest enemy, and as a parent, you then have to constantly prevent it. You have to protect the ego you helped to build up.

This is not to say that kids need to be left to face failure alone. What kids need most is an attentive parent. An attentive parent believes that their child can accomplish great things through hard work and perseverance, not intelligence or beauty. Attentiveness is not the same as doting. Attentive parents are those who pay attention to the struggles of their child, see their suffering and their failure, and then come alongside and help them get up. Your goal as a parent isn't to make them happy, to keep them from fussing or from feeling sad. Life is full of failure and sadness. Your goal is to help them face such pain with strength and character.

CHAPTER 4

ATTENTION SEEKING

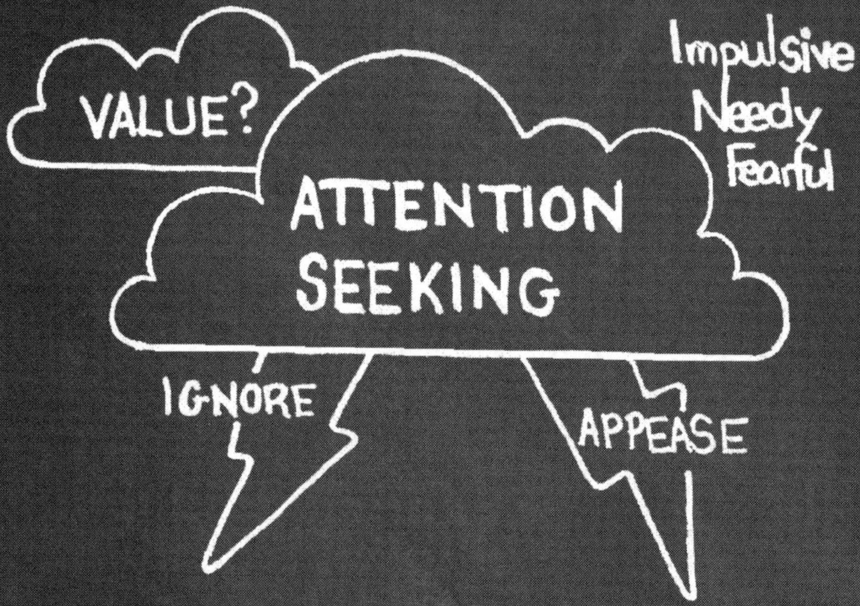
VALUE?
ATTENTION SEEKING
Impulsive
Needy
Fearful
IGNORE
APPEASE

THE QUESTION OF VALUE

Psychologists have long theorized about what it takes to motivate people. The one that resonates strongest with the work I've done was developed by David McClelland. He lists three main motives: Control, Connectedness, and Accomplishment. People want to control and influence others, belong to a group, and accomplish a goal. Each person is impacted differently by these internal drives, and I believe that they each speak to a fundamental question we all ask: do I matter. When it comes to our children, we have to ask ourselves to what degree that question is unresolved. The answer will determine whether those motivations serve to build them up or tear them down.

The question of value is answered in two main ways: the work you do and the relationships you maintain. Our most common fears (rejection and failure) show us the way to resolve this need for value. Once the fundamental need for safety is accounted for, people fear being useless and worthless above all. These two avenues are the only real ways you can resolve your question, if that's even possible. Unfortunately, no matter how successful or popular you may become, the question doesn't leave you alone. That also means there are some really unhealthy ways that people try to resolve it. If you can control the people you love and the work you do, then perhaps you can be free from fear, but your quest to control your unanswerable fear will poison the things you do and the love you share.

The more healthy our relationships are with the people most important to us, the freer we are to simply be ourselves. Those relationships can be with parents, siblings, or friends. Teachers and other mentors can also fill that spot for a time. For many people, celebrities sit strangely in that place too, especially with the way social media makes us feel as though we really know them. For most people on earth and for most of history, God is also one of those important conections, no matter how far off he may seem. It's not insignificant that we want our behavior, and thus our very selves, to be approved by the one who made all things.

Your connection with a spiritual ideal affects the way you connect with the people in your life. That's only true, of course, to the degree that your ideals have been integrated into your deepest self. Your words matter very little in the long run, simply because the part of you that agrees with ideas is such a small part of who you are. To genuinely integrate a belief into yourself, you have to navigate all the layers of yourself. That takes time and dedication, and that work will spread into every relationship and purpose you pursue. The healthiest marriages and families don't focus on unanswerable fear and endlessly controlling one another. The same can be said for the best work environments.

Our children face the same question of value from the moment they are born. For children who are not noticed at a young age, severe damage is done to their ability to connect with other people. Fear takes over. However, our kids' lives don't have to be traumatizing for them to be hungry for the satisfaction of being valued. For young children, attentive love, especially of a mother, will do much to quiet the needy and impulsive acting out that plagues so many children. For older kids, the demanding love of a father becomes pivotal as they establish strength of character. Kids who are missing attentive and demanding parents will grow accustomed to big swings of emotion that establish a pattern for all their future relationships.

Research and experience show us the destructive pattern of parents who are consistently critical of their children's flaws, who are often absent when kids are home, or who ignore them in favor of their own emotional distractions. These parents get children who don't believe that they matter. Being valuable is a fundamental need, and they hunger for it. As they grow up hungry, they accelerate their emotions and behavior in a bid for relevance in the lives of busy and distracted adults. Hunger is the right word, I believe, because adults often think kids are plotting to gain attention. You don't plot to have that cookie in the break room when you walk by, but it sure is hard to say no to it. I think the desire for value is so deeply set in our hearts that impulsive and fearful behavior begins to spring out of that longing when we least expect it. It can shift our whole personality.

That attention-seeking mind-set is closely linked to difficulty kids have with paying attention to things in school. Every teacher will tell you that the attention seeker isn't just showing off, they actually can't follow more than one step of directions. Over time, they fall behind academically. They can't pay attention to the annoyance their peers are communicating, and they can't change their behavior even if they wanted to. The fact is, these kids want to change. They want to be liked and regarded by peers, especially as they enter adolescence when their friends and classmate take on the primary influence role in their lives. They want what they can't have as their needy emotional state sabotages their ability to connect.

They end up gathering together with the other kids who are struggling to enjoy meaningful friendship. Those friend groups quickly become frenemies: best friends today and hating each other tomorrow. Some parents go so far as to move schools and even homes to get away from such friend groups, and that can work sometimes, but often they end up with the same type of friends at the new school. It's a friend group who are all hungry for something.

It's important for young parents to know they have limited time to make an impact on their children. When your child hits puberty, your days of primary influence are numbered. If they are in middle school and still hunger to know if they matter to you, they will start to search for it elsewhere. You can still turn the boat, but it will be a struggle. We'll talk more about that process in future chapters, but just know that it gets harder. Perhaps you're already in that struggle. There's hope, but you're going to have to grow as much as they are.

It's no easy feat helping your children deal with their own question of value, their fear that they don't matter, and their need for attention from adults and peers. It starts with you dealing with your own question, and it's time for you to choose growth and cooperation over fear and control. When there are disagreements and disappointments, even chaos in your household, what kind of environment will you establish? Will it be one that demands obedience and uses anger to enforce it? Will it be an emotional rollercoaster of shame and rejection? It's time to set your ideal higher, first for yourself and then with your children. It's time to make your home a place where parents and children can grow up to be themselves.

ADAM AND EVE

Since we're pondering the big questions in life, it seems right to pause and reflect on the biggest of them all: God. A simple but useful definition of God is the embodiment of every ideal. He is the most loving of all the loving people you've known, the purest hearted, the best provider, the strongest protector, the most just, the most patient. In so doing, he becomes both universal and timeless. Such ideals are best expressed in stories that have been told and retold long before there were movies or books in which to consume them. It's easy to see why narratives are the centerpiece of every culture. The heroes that fill your community's stories are living out your ideals in some important way.

In your life, you've had events that resonated with you so powerfully that you found yourself telling those stories again and again. Perhaps you've heard some of these stories from others, but you still pass them on as your own discovered truth. They didn't even happen to you, but you still retell them. Now imagine such a story was so important that your children told it after you died. Of all such stories, there are a few that get passed on for generations. A few of those stories spread outside of family or community and begin to impact people around the world, getting retold in different cultures and times.

These stories become the basis for scriptures of all kind, and no matter what your views are about any religion (or all of them), we should take seriously something that has been so impactful to so many people. One of the oldest of these stories is that of Adam and Eve. So many people have resonated with this story that it has covered the earth. Adam and Eve are present in most the major religious traditions over many centuries. Regardless of your opinion on the historical nature of such a tale, there is a truth being told in it that should not be ignored.

The first married couple resided in a walled garden, protected from the wild world outside. They were given work to do, and they were literally made for each other. Their question of value was answered by God himself, who walked with them in the cool of the morning. Into that protected and cooperative environment came a single question. No walls could keep this snake from coming in. This question pulled their hearts away from the highest spiritual ideal and separated them from each other.

The question was one of value. If you eat of the forbidden fruit, the serpent whispered, you can take into your hands the knowledge of whether you are good or bad, valuable or worthless, useful or a failure. You'll answer your question, and you'll do it on your own. You can be in control, you can be like God. And when you eat it, you'll know the good and the evil within you. You'll judge others' value, their goodness, without even trying. You'll compare yourself to everyone. Is this starting to sound familiar?

The first people fell into the same struggle that we, with all our modern amenities and ambitions, continue to face. How can we be good? How can we be important? How do we find our value? When we raise kids, we have to see that they too will be asking this question, and we have the opportunity to set them on a path back to cooperation and trust. This is why the easiest way to connect with a kid is to simply pay attention to them. Notice their shoes are like yours or their dress is new. Compliment their haircut or the drawing they made. Look them in the eyes when you do it, and you'll have someone attached to you with a purity that is hard to rival.

In that connection, you've quieted their question of value for just a moment, and they will keep coming back for more. As an adult, you're not unlike God in their eyes: an ideal that they are longing to emulate. If you handle this well, you can create a place in their lives to have a positive influence. In my experience, even the kids who arrive at school from safe environments still face this question. As five- and six-year-olds, they may not be struggling against it, but every child will ask if they matter to you. That's part of their efforts to see if they can trust you.

For others, their home life is chaos and a struggle every day to get their needs met. The more crisis they live in, the more burning is the question of value. When the adults they live with can't get their own lives in order, when they don't have the emotional strength or skill to handle what life brings, children experience that as being worthless. I wasn't worth paying attention to. The more crisis a child grows up in, the harder it is to cooperate and trust the people in their lives.

IMPULSIVE, NEEDY, FEARFUL

When anyone feels worthless for a long period of time, especially young kids, they become fearful, emotionally needy, and impulsive. They struggle to make plans and complete them. They can't pay attention to more than two or three steps in a row without reminder. Their unconscious needs are tugging at the fringes of their thoughts, always hungry for attention and thus value from important people. They're embarrassed easily but can't stop doing ridiculous things to show off. They can't maintain healthy friendships because they set themselves up as the victim and focus on life's unfairness. They feel so entitled to the affection and attention of others that it starts the seeds of resentment toward a world where other people's lives seem easy in comparison. They think they are owed something because they hunger for it so intensely.

It's worth repeating that these people, especially as kids, sit in contrast to the child who is doted upon and sees other people as owing them attention because they are superior. The child whose parents show them empathy at every turn, prioritizing their feelings with outsized protective instincts to avoid disappointment and rejection, ironically never learns to care for others. Instead, they see themselves as little royalty who deserve to be served by others. They aren't being taught compassion, they are on their way to being tyrants. Compassion is taught by seeing the harsh consequences of your selfishness, not by focusing on your own feelings. A lesson on compassion says, "Look what you did. How does that make them (not you) feel?"

Both the ignored and the doted upon child feel the world is unfair when they don't get what they want, and they will both resent the world eventually. Their problem is that they each think their emotional needs are the most important thing in their world. The neglected and the appeased both end up in the same fate: their ego takes the center stage of their lives. In schools, we see many kids in this state of self-centeredness, and it is getting worse.

Where once the 40-year veteran teachers would talk about the impact of TV on the minds of kids, it's no longer a decades long transformation. Today, teachers in the classroom less than 10 years can tell you how differently the kids now think and feel, how fragile and distracted they are becoming. The first iPad was released just under 10 years ago. iPhones came out three years before that. A decade of smart phone and tablet immersion.

We call it an attention-seeking mind-set, and it's no simple thing to overcome, especially when you're trying to teach reading, writing, math, and science along the way. Teachers have collected a large number of strategies at every level to handle such kids. Quite often they grow out of it, they mature, but if the fundamental question of value isn't dealt with, then they may grow into something much worse.

If a child came to school without having eaten, they would struggle mightily to pay attention. Their physical hunger would distract them and make them grumpy and easily off task. For kids in an attention-seeking mind-set, their hunger is emotional, but it is just as powerful. When teachers work with these kids, they set them up front or on the edge of the room so there are fewer kids to distract them. They check in with them multiple times during each lesson and assume that when directions are given, those kids weren't listening. They teach them explicitly what other kids figure out on their own. All these strategies, and there are many more, are really just different ways of paying attention to kids who are starving for value. It's the only way we can get to the job of teaching, and when half your class comes to school hungry in this way, it can completely shift how much academics a class is able to cover in a year.

I often hear people complain about our failing school systems. I don't see it. I see teachers dealing with so many emotionally hungry kids that there's not enough attention to go around. Educational spending has risen steadily over the last five decades in America, and performance has not. Much of that is spent on ill-informed and idealistic programs, but just as much, perhaps more, is spent to equip teachers to deal with ever increasing emotional starvation.

ATTENTION DEFICIT DISORDER

In the 90's, you would often hear about the crisis of fatherhood in America. Deadbeat dads were seen as the cause of so many of society's ills. As far as I can tell, the number of involved fathers hasn't increased measurably since that time, but I can tell you that that's not the trend we see any more. What we see happening today is young kids coming to school without attentive mothers. They might be present in the home, though it's not unusual for them not to be, but they're not engaged. Too many moms are staring at their phones while their kids cry out for attention. They're trading up to a new boyfriend or leaving kids with grandparents for extended periods of time. What do we do when both fathers *and* mothers are falling down on the job? As educators, we pick up the pieces of their children who long to matter to someone. This job is too big and too vital to be left to school teachers alone. Communities need to come together and build their own solutions.

Kids with an involved father and attentive mother are, by and large, bored in class and far ahead academically. This is a powerful reality as a parent. If you can resolve your child's need for attention and value, you are giving them a significant head start in life. Structured bedtime routines, family dinners, screen free weekdays: these things are nearly impossible to maintain if only one parent is invested. They also get your child ahead academically.

Every time you encounter that needy response from your child, will you ignore it because "They just want attention"? You wouldn't do that if they were hungry for food. Or will you follow them around, protecting them from disappointment and rejection, valuing their hurt feelings above all. "Narrow is the way that leads to life, and few find it." Few indeed.

There's growing evidence that a child's ability to pay attention is impacted by how much they have been paid attention to: their question of value. There is undoubtedly a physical component to the condition, and I have seen medications produce incredibly helpful results in the short term. At the same time, every teacher can tell you about kids who live in disorganized households who have a disorganized way of thinking. When parents go through divorce, for example, not only do the symptoms of ADD increase, but they can form long-term patterns of thought. There are even studies showing brief exposure to chaotic TV shows like SpongeBob can create symptoms of attention deficit in children who have never shown signs before.

It was well documented in the 1990's that there was a sharp increase in the number of kids who struggle to pay attention. Doctors and educators call it Attention Deficit Disorder, and it's considered a disability according to federal law. What you may not know is that ADD and ADHD diagnoses, and medication prescriptions, have continued to increased at a staggering pace. Between 2007 and 2011, the number of diagnoses increased 50%.* Parents and teachers have struggled to accommodate within the confines of the classroom in such a way that these kids can succeed.

The effects aren't just academic. Kids with attention difficulties struggle socially as well. They miss the cues their peers are sending that signal when to stop doing something that might have been funny before. They sit in the middle of circles when everyone is on the edge. They're often seen as annoying and immature, and many of these kids are aware of these opinions but also struggle to care about them.

---

* http://cdc.gov/ncbddd/adhd/data.html

Of the many symptoms and skill deficits, which are the most important? Is there one skill that if learned would create a positive effect across multiple areas? Russell A. Barkley, PhD, an experienced clinician, researcher, and author, has an interesting take on understanding the primary struggle that these kids are facing. He calls ADHD not attention deficit, but intention deficit: "They're blind to the future." These kids cannot make plans and complete them, and in that description he's found an effective method of addressing the condition even at an early age—what psychologists call executive functioning.

Executive functioning just means the ability to pause and make a decision that's contrary to your initial impulse. The initial impulses are almost always selfish. When you teach them to stop their tantrum or eat the food they're scared will taste bad or share their toy, you're strengthening the part of their brain that can stop and think. It's important to realize that you're not teaching them in the way one might think of teaching them a math fact. It's also not just a bad habit they have, though that's closer to reality. They have patterns of thought and strength of character that have to be established with consistent feedback and loving conflict. Help them get strong.

Both my experience and my conversations with other educators support Dr. Barkley's conclusions. It might also explain why research has shown kids with involved dads are far less likely to have ADD. Dads seem to be more likely to enforce task completion and rigid sets of expectations. In fact, the impact of such fathers is widespread and dramatic. According to research, kids who have dads that don't ignore them gain in many ways:

- They're less likely to commit suicide

- More able to postpone gratification, a huge predictor of college and career success

- More likely to report positive emotional health, even in the face of significant trauma

- Less likely to be addicted to pornography and video games in early adulthood and beyond

The list goes on and on.

One can even follow this path of lack of attention from their dad down the road that many teenagers travel: toward shame and aimlessness. When kids have not learned to postpone gratification in order to acquire a real skill that makes them useful, they begin to realize that girls aren't interested in them. They can't measure up to the successful student leaders around them who might be athletic or socially more adept than them. No one understands them, and their failures only reinforce that it's not just certain kids who've rejected them, but society at large. It's not hard to understand where that resentment can lead for a few kids who are also fascinated with violence and an overwhelming longing to be recognized. Though few venture far down that road, at its end is the mentality of a school shooter.

CHAPTER 5

BIRTH OF A POWER-STRUGGLER

For anyone who sees their value as the primary need in their life, it will always get in the way of their relationships and their work. No matter how well you raise your children, there will come a time when your kids begin to shift their mind-set from impulsive, needy, and fearful into something even worse: a struggle for power and control. Traditionally, we have attributed this phase of development to the onslaught of hormones that come with middle school, but that has not been my experience. Though every child visits this mind-set, some get stuck.

What I've seen, as I've worked with middle schoolers, high schoolers, and elementary students, is that all kids become more aware of their strengths and weaknesses as they grow up and begin to compare themselves to others. If you combine that with some kind of crisis of value, they shift their mind-set from feeling needy and vulnerable to feeling angry and powerful. Whereas they might have looked to you for value before, in adolescence they start to give up on that strategy. Much of that is healthy independence, but as they begin to see how they don't measure up a fire kindles inside them to not be ignored. The effective strategies we're looking at will help you handle the power struggle so your children don't get stuck.

Where the attention-seeker is impulsive, the power struggling mentality is more deliberate. Some kids predominantly struggle with others:

their peers and authority figures. Their hunger is no longer about value, but control. Their misbehavior begins to be timed for effectiveness, and they look for the place where the fewest adults are present. At other times they struggle with themselves, and they make rules in order to feel like they are succeeding in having command over something and compensate for their weakness and failure. They're all looking for ways to stay in control, and they go through a cycle of struggle between themselves and others in a pattern that looks a lot like a pendulum.

As a principal, my first task for each kid is to get to know them. If you don't have a rough impression of their state of mind, you don't know how to handle their behaviors. A defiant rule-breaker has vastly different needs from the impulsive but remorseful child. Some kids lie to get away with things, while others will lie to avoid disappointing you. You get impressions of kids and think of them as pleasers, rule-followers, attention-seekers, or work-avoiders. Some fly low under the radar but they've got their own schemes. Others are introverted and still want to be noticed. You see their little personalities each time they interact with their teachers or chat with their friends, and for the first few years at the elementary level, I felt I had a good sense of the kids.

In the sixth year of the job, however, something changed my outlook forever. As part of a small community, our kids tend to stay in our school for all six years of elementary. Not only did I get to know them really well, but I began to see the same kids do something unexpected: they changed categories. In each grade, several kids were sent to me in second and third grade for being impulsive and hungry for attention. They disrupt class to be funny or bossy. Over time, many kids transitioned into patterns of deliberate, aggressive misbehavior, and the worse off a kid had it at home, the faster they made this shift. This was something I didn't see in teaching middle and high school.

FROM FEAR TO ANGER

I have worked with some kids, and admittedly they're rare, who get stuck in this aggressive mentality so severely that it destroys them.

Their relationships with peers are plagued with accusation and blame, they push against authority so much that they can't receive help or even learn from their mistakes, and they lose the ability to get any meaningful work done. If you can't learn or get to work, how on earth will you ever find meaning in your work? The unresolved question of value morphs into a subtext of victimhood and bitterness. The fruit of these beliefs is an intense aggression.

When these kids were kindergartners and first graders, their neediness and fear would drive them to such a degree that they couldn't hear anything but love or hate. Everyone was either their best friend or their worst enemy, and often it will be the same teacher, student, or principal (and all in the same day). For these kids, it was only the most powerful personalities who could break through, and the only friends they could make were the kids who also pestered and resisted.

The act of watching my teachers patiently construct boundaries crushed my idealistic fantasies about these kids. It would take far more than a few weeks of patient affection to work miracles on them. This was a multi-year process. And in that time I did see progress for a few kids. The hard part is watching those kids, who are often raised in the most chaotic environment, move away as soon as you seem to be making progress. If we couldn't get through to them, their fear of abandonment and constant failure to live up to any expectations wrought a transformation in their hearts. They covered their fears with anger. People stopped being a source of fulfillment and became objects to control or avoid. They were either in your control or in your way. People were sheep or wolves, and those kids knew they had to be wolves if they were going to survive.

Those kids are a rarity, however, and for many classes in my small school, there were no such kiddos. Instead it was your standard goofballs and happy-go-lucky children. It was for one such class that I was pulling the data for misbehavior from the information system we keep. This was a group of fifth graders I had known since they were five, and who were chatty but friendly overall. Very quickly it became clear in the numbers that these older kids were all getting in trouble at the same time of day: lunchtime.

When kids get in trouble, we always take note of when and where the infractions take place. I had to ask myself why this chatty but friendly group would be having such distinct problems. What is lunchtime missing that the rest of the day isn't? Their teachers. At that time, we had other staff from different parts of the building supervising lunch so classroom teachers can have a break for lunch. These fifth graders were waiting to be away from the adults who could really make the punishments stick. It wasn't just impulsivity, it was on purpose.

Having watched these kids grow up, I had an impression of their attitudes as a group. They were immature for their age, but generally easygoing and kind. For the first time I saw them differently, and it alarmed me. I had always assumed that the personality of the group stayed roughly the same. But now I was seeing changes, and it set me thinking. I had to figure out what changed. When I dug down into which kids were actually misbehaving, I was shocked. The same kids who were impulsive and likeable as eight-year-olds were the ones who began to turn on each other as eleven-year-olds with aggression and deliberate defiance.

CRISIS MEETS COMPARISON

What started this change? This piece took me awhile to narrow down. I remembered my own changes growing up and where my insecurities started to really change how I thought of myself. What were the events and ideas that made those changes stick? I distinctly remember being a student in sixth grade social studies. I was sitting on the left side of the room during some free time watching the other boys crowd around a kid named Brian. Brian's dad was a lawyer, and that meant he got the latest Air Jordans. This was 1989, and for the boys in my sixth grade class, few things made you cooler than what sort of sneakers you were wearing. Not much has changed, I guess.

When I looked down at my own shoes, the Payless knock-off sneakers that my family could afford, I remember the sinking feeling that there was something better about him, and that I didn't measure up. That feeling sent me into myself, hoping no one would see that I wasn't worthy. Now that I am and an adult, watching these kids begin this same journey of insecurity, I saw that the crisis of value and comparison had combined forces in their hearts to betray them. My struggle as a kid had mostly been internal, but it was a struggle nonetheless: a struggle for power over how people saw me and how I saw myself. Other people respond to their crisis of value by struggling against the people around them, but the comparison and control that took over were different symptoms of the same disease.

Not long after running that data on those fifth graders and their lunchtime antics, I was watching a Netflix documentary on Tony Robbins, of all people. If you don't know who he is, he is a successful life coach and inspirational speaker. He's been on TV for what seems like decades, so I was a bit embarrassed to be watching this overly excited loud talker do his thing on stage. Once I looked beyond the hype, however, I found that he was actually making sense. He was talking about how psychologists seem to agree that everyone has a few basic needs: loving relationships, certainty, variety, and significance. To those fundamentals Tony adds two more: contribution and growth. However, it matters a lot which of these needs is in the driver's seat of your life. If certainty (control) and significance are your highest priorities, they will become toxic. When I heard this, I started taking notes. These kids were on my mind.

Because these kids were missing the fundamental sense that they have value, they were insecure. They hadn't mattered enough to their parents to be paid attention to and disciplined in such a way that they weren't always failing. That hunger for meaning and discipline had been destroying their potential and they knew it. And the more they knew it, and the more they saw other kids get what they were missing, it was like a switch was thrown in their hearts. They were going to take control.

I shared my ideas withour behavior consultant and friend of mine, Mark Summers. Mark has worked with troubled kids for decades in several small school districts including our own, and we have sat many times in my office to talk about kids, how they work, and how to give them what they need to succeed. When I was formulating these ideas into my big flow chart his decades of supporting kids not only resulted in very similar insights, but he saw them play out across multiple generations in small towns around our region.

Mark characterized these power struggling kids in this way: "If you won't give me the value I need, then I'm going to take it for myself. I will not be ignored." And in that moment, these kids were adding onto their need for value a larger need: control. They were switching who was in the driver's seat. Seeking attention had left them always hungry for more. They were going to have to feed themselves.

INTERNAL CHAOS
REQUIRES EXTERNAL CONTROL

For the 12-year-old me, the crisis of comparison was about money and cool shoes. Because the difference wasn't as significant in my case, that change of drive from value to control didn't happen until I was twelve. For many reasons, not least of which is simply my personality, I focused most of that desire for control on myself. For the kids I care for as a principal, it was hitting them at a younger age (some much younger). I think the biggest difference comes down to how much chaos each child is experiencing in their life. When a crisis combines with comparison to peers, a desire for power and control steps in to make you feel safe.

External chaos, especially if it feels close to what matters to you, has a big impact on the internal state of your mind. If you've ever needed to clean the house in order to sit down and write or read or think, then perhaps you can relate. This cycle of chaos, value, and control doesn't stop when you become an adult (whenever that is). The more chaotic your thoughts and feelings are, the more external control you will find yourself needing. That's why writing out your plans and intentions for your life can be so transformative. Dr. Jordan Peterson, a psychologist and researcher at the University of Toronto, describes it like a roadmap. When you set your aim and make your efforts and ambitions line up accordingly, it's like bringing order to the chaos of your thoughts and emotions.

The more out of balance you feel, the more you lean away from that chaos. The problem in life is that the leaning creates a new problem all it's own. It's like sitting on a swing set and then leaning back. Leaning one way only pushes you toward the other extreme. Even if you don't mean to, momentum and gravity work to get you going in the other direction. Your effort to lean one way works for a time, but you will always find yourself swinging back toward the thing you tried to avoid. We react by leaning still more, and we swing higher and higher each time.

In this case, it isn't physics at work, but the need for value and control you naturally feel. You begin to fight against your question of value, but soon you're swinging back against others. The fight comes from your need for control combined with the rebellious nature that all people share. Eventually—and we've all felt this at times—you will actually begin to rebel against yourself. And the pendulum swings ever higher.

So I watched as kids fell into the struggle for power, and the more I saw this progression and its symptoms, the more I saw them in myself and the adults around me. When I looked at history and politics, I started to see it there. We have a country divided into the politics of blaming others for our problems or shaming the individual. We take turns letting each side of the battle lead for a time, but we soon become collectively tired of the struggle in one direction and swing back to the other.

Even when I traveled to Indonesia and Africa to meet with pastors and teachers, they said they saw the same things in adults and kids alike. I've been able to bring these ideas to some of the poorest places on earth, with centuries of poverty and corruption at every level of society. Everywhere I go, and with nearly all the conflict I see between both kids and adults, there is a strong element in one and all to gain power and control over yourself and others. Shame and blame are always at work. That's partly why I feel it is so fundamental to the human story that I would bring in ancient stories. There's something universal here.

DOMINATION, JUDGMENT

When the struggle for power aims itself at others, whether authority figures or peers have become the targets, the symptoms are the same.

The most well-known in schools is the stereotypical domination that "bullies" display. In the time I've worked with such kids in high school all the way down to kindergarten and preschool, bullies don't discriminate between adults and peers. They aren't calling kids names because they're different, and they don't talk back to adults because those adults aren't kind enough. They want power over you, and whatever button they can push to get it, they will.

The most basic form of domination is emotional. If I can deliberately get another person upset, then I've controlled them at a very basic level, and my power over them proves, for a few seconds at least, that I'm above them. If you're a parent of a teenager, you've felt the prod of this mentality when the defiant "Why?" gets thrown in your face for the umpteenth time.

I put the word "bully" in quotations because the behavior is far more widespread than the mean kid you think of when you hear the word. That kid got stuck in the same cycle that most everyone has been in. The problem I've encountered as a principal is that parents and kids will use the word to mean anything rude or mean that may happen to them. I'd say that 90% of the incidents parents call about, demanding justice for the bullying that's been going on for months, is actually just rudeness or a generally mean kid. To label rudeness or mean behavior as targeted aggression just adds emotional baggage to an already complicated situation.

Researchers define real bullying as the use of aggression to target someone to exert power over them: intentionally and repeatedly making someone feel small so that you feel big. What it isn't is being a bossy kid. A bully isn't the rude kid who annoys people on purpose. Both of those are, however, signs of someone in an early form of power struggling, and left unattended or uncorrected, it will get worse.

What researchers on the subject have also concluded is that the most powerful tactic for schools isn't to teach about diversity, though that doesn't hurt. The vast majority of kids and adults have something about them that can be the target of insult or jest, something that makes them different. The topic of the jokes and jabs doesn't actually matter. They are just testing to see who will back down and cower.

Those who appease or bow down will become targets for future attack. Every tyrant loathes the one who appeases them. Therefore, the most effective thing your kids can do is resist the impulse to freeze up and give in. The "bully" wants to know if your kid is another predator, or are they prey. Remember that the power struggler inherently believes that everyone is either a sheep or a wolf. The sad consequence of such belief is that there is no room for heroes or loving generosity or trust. The more you see your child struggle for control (or the more that you do it) the more you'll see them push trusting relationships away. There are only people I can control and people I hate.

Boldness and calm confidence is a powerful response to the power struggles they will encounter, but it's no easy thing to teach your child. Confidence can only come from real success in the face of potential failure, and the deeply held belief that they are worthy of love and belonging. That belief gives birth to freedom from needy attention seeking or getting dragged into the same power struggle as your opponent. The desire for a cutting reply to every insult is only your own ego driving you into the conflict. That's why kindness in the face of such insults is the gold standard. If you have the ability to destroy your enemy, but you give them kindness instead, you have risen above the struggle for domination.

The fuel for social and physical domination among kids is the audience that always gathers. Dominators always want a crowd, and if the crowd is silent, it gets interpreted as approval, even if it's really cowering. If a whole crowd is silent, both the aggressor and the target come to believe that they are rooting for the aggressor. In fact, the majority of the crowd is afraid they'll be the next target, but it doesn't matter. Now the power struggling kid has dominated the whole room, and anyone who doesn't approve is another sheep who needs to be dominated.

One really effective school-wide program I've helped institute was training for the bystanders in such cases. If kids are circled around a display of aggression in the hall or class, and one or two bold leaders are able to stand with the target, it changes the whole dynamic. I heard a great story of such an incident at the high school level. A new kid had become the target of a power struggler in the hall, and the quarterback of the football team walked right up to the kid getting targeted, stood next to him and faced the aggressor. "We don't do that here" is all he said. In that moment, the whole circle of spectators dissolved, and the aggressor slinked away in shame. What a powerful display of leadership and courage.

Another common symptom of a power struggling mentality is trying to be right all the time. It's a lower level of domination that many kids crave, especially boys. Here's a fun example: get together with a group of brothers and their friends. The brother without a friend present may start to feel the lack of value and choose to struggle to regain his position. He'll try to show his value by controlling what is talked about and what activities will happen next. Listen closely to their conversations without being noticed, if you can manage it, and within a few minutes, you'll hear them correcting each other and fact-checking every word. In our house, we call it being a know-it-all. As a sixth grade teacher, it was constant in my math classes. Kids would often glory in doing it to me as the highest status person in the room. I started to repeat, "Don't forget, being a know-it-all isn't the same as being smart."

Power struggle doesn't always follow this model, however. When I was in school, I dominated by getting the highest score on the math test and subtly making sure everyone knew it. I wasn't bragging around the class (at least I don't remember it that way), but I also wasn't keeping anything secret. For the folks whose disposition tends toward struggling with yourself, success/comparison is their own version of domination. Control as a means of gaining value.

REBELLION AND BLAME

The second main symptom of the struggle for control over others is rebellion and indulgence. If dominating says that someone else deserves what they get, then rebellion says "I deserve to get what I want." Perhaps what you want is to sneak out of work early, or have too much wine or ice cream. The indulging tastes sweetest when someone has told you not to have it, even if that someone is you. You know you're rationalizing your rebellion when you start saying, "I had a stressful day," or some such thing. Taken to extremes, eating disorders and alcohol abuse are not far away. No one ends up at compulsion without going through the first steps of rebellion and indulgence. Rationalizing is an important point, and it's a good indicator that you or your child are heading toward the pendulum. Everyone has an inner lawyer on retainer to justify why your mistakes either aren't your fault or aren't that bad. "I wasn't hurting anyone," you tell yourself, but the cycle is beginning. You're choosing control, instead of personal or relational health. Instead of processing your own question of value, you're going down a road and forming a habit that is intensely hard to break.

Habits are some of the most powerful means by which you can transform your life, but they all spring from beliefs you hold about yourself or others. That's why the most significant interventions take so long to work. If you want to turn around the life of a kid, it is almost always a multi-year process. Every year of my work as a school principal, I can list the five kids with whom I've spent countless hours. In the first or second year of such work, there is almost no sign of impact, and it's always heartbreaking when they move away. It's the third and fourth year of speaking the truth in patience and firmness that you see the facade start to crack.

If you want to transition your own life or marriage, it's the same. It will take years of changing habits and the beliefs that sit underneath each one. What are the excuses you're using, and what are the insecurities and bitterness that are keeping you stuck in the same cycles? If you talk yourself out of dealing with the problems within, your inner lawyer will make sure you end up being declared innocent. The problem is that you will never feel innocent, and your shame will send you deeper into the pendulum swing.

THE VICTIM MENTALITY

The last big symptom of a power-struggler that I want to cover in this chapter is the game of blame and victimhood. This habit is so pervasive and destructive that it deserves a chapter of its own, but that's for another book. A victim mentality can take an emotionally healthy, creative child, and send them spiraling into dysfunction. The hardest part about it is that it's fundamentally a belief about yourself and the world, so it can be very difficult to reverse. When your child has a bad habit they need patient reminders, but what do you do when the way they look at the world is all wrong?

The victim mentality is very close to the self-righteous political or religious zealot. They both see themselves as having the moral high ground, but one is focused on strengths and the other on weaknesses. Fundamentally, they both end up in the same place all power-strugglers go: the dismantling of purposeful work and the shallowing of relationships. That's not to say that blaming others for your problems will push people away. In fact, you will draw like-minded friends to you very quickly. But none of those friends will have a sense that they can make an actual change in their world because they fundamentally see themselves as powerless.

The draw of the blame game is that you feel righteous in your martyrdom because nothing is your fault. And even if it was your fault, your guilt pails in comparison to the wrong you've suffered. Each successive slight you receive will build upon the last until you begin to see the whole world arrayed against you. Victim thinking is what leads to destructive outbursts of many kinds, made by kids who seem jaded or angry. The world deserves what it gets, or so the thinking will take you in the end. Some even set out to give the world its due.

You may think this mentality is mostly for teenagers, but I've met 8-year-olds who had already gathered a whole set of blaming beliefs. One child I've worked with would rehearse different phrases and arguments whenever she was in trouble. I would hear her preparing her arguments like a highly trained attorney about to cross-examine the witness. In this case, I was the witness, and that blame game was aimed at me most of the time. This kid could apply blame to everyone around her no matter what bad behavior she was guilty of. Her power struggling was so intense, that she could slam a door in your face, try to kick you in the leg, then begin crying within minutes saying you had done those very things to her.

In my experience, the most destructive symptom of a power struggling mind-set isn't bullying, manipulation, or rebellion. It is the victim mentality. Playing the victim will suck the meaning out of every relationship it touches and the joy from every worthwhile endeavor. For most of us, we play the victim as an excuse after having made a mistake. It's the cover for something impulsive or foolish that we've done. Eventually, if you let it, it will weave its way into your thinking about everything.

That form of nihilism is appealing in the same way that an unemployed teenage summer might be. No responsibility feels like freedom, but the consequence of thinking that nothing you do matters is that everyone needs to matter. Your version of freedom betrays you in the end. When you grow up and realize that you want to matter to someone, maybe even to lots of people, your deeply held victimhood won't let you go. What do kids need who are stuck in this despair? They need someone to bring them their share of the blame, which is another way of saying responsibility. In so doing, there is a true purpose.

CHAPTER 6

POWER-STRUGGLING MENTALITY

went to a professional development training for teachers, school counselors, and principals recently about how the brain is affected by trauma, especially long-term "toxic" stress. One of the activities we covered was the thought patterns traumatized kids have about their world. We each filled in the blanks based on the kids we know and the conversations we've had with them. As you might expect, in a room full of people trying to intervene in the lives of kids who struggle in school, the insight was clear and consistent. On a sheet of paper, we were asked to fill in the thought bubbles our struggling kids have about themselves, other people, and the world.

Teachers, principals, and counselors around the room shared with each other heartbreaking stories about kids whose thoughts pour out in moments of rage and humiliation. In those moments, kids say shockingly similar things about themselves. "I'm stupid," "I can't do anything right," and "I'm worthless." We had all heard kids use these phrases, and no amount of reassurance at that moment will stop the flood of negative self talk those kids are feeling.

If you ask those kids later, when they're not upset, if they still believe those things about themselves, you hear a very different story. They will tell you all the things you want to hear. The question is, which one is the truth. Are the thoughts that come up when you're angry what you "really" think? When you're calm and you say what you believe, is it just to make yourself or others happy? Are you just saying the "right" answer to avoid more conflict? It's hard to tell, but what is clear is that people of all ages are finding themselves in conflict within their own minds about their own value.

When kids who've been through struggles and chaos look at other people, the ones who seem to have a perfect life, they're not sad, or at least not for long. They're jealous and angry. Those people don't deserve the good things they've received, and the struggling kid doesn't deserve the struggle. It's not fair. In the midst of that struggle, either no one will help, which makes them complicit in the suffering, or no one is able to help, which makes them useless and powerless. Everyone is either causing their suffering or useless to stop it. The world is made up of sheep and wolves.

The same ideas echoed throughout this seminar full of dedicated people working with struggling kids: someone needs to intervene in the lives of kids in crisis and comparison by showing them a third way. Not just the way of the victim and the perpetrator, but one of power and mercy, strength and forgiveness, love and authority. If no one does that, then those kids will almost certainly begin to see everyone as either a person to be controlled or someone to be despised. After all, if the world is made up of predators and prey, who would choose to be prey? Only the fool or the coward.

The third category of thoughts we were writing down was interesting: how do these kids think about the world around them? How do kids see the world, and how is it different than their view of other people? The participants in the training filled this category with words like "unfair," and "unsafe," and a bunch of versions of meaningless. "Why try?" is the common refrain once these kids reach a certain age. I kept thinking of the Power Struggling Mind-set in the kids I know who've grown out of needing others and decided to take control of their need for value.

What struck me about this third category is not just that it's an extension of the "Other People" into generalities, but also that how you think about the world is very similar to how you think about God himself. Perhaps this could even be generalized to most religious structures. Faith teachings are a means to explain the pain we suffer as meaningful, and therefore God himself (however you define such a being) is either benevolent in the face of a broken world, or absent because of it. Very often those who reject faith, do so as an expression of the view that such a God is either a sheep, and therefore no God at all, or a wolf who should not be revered. Our view of God is not just an expression of our beliefs, but a result of the longing we each have to explain our pain.

The more pain we suffer, and the less help we receive in the face of it, doesn't just change what we believe, but how our brain is wired. A big part of this class called Collaborative Problem Solving was about the research in neuroscience explaining the way trauma changes the brain. There is a lot in it, but the shortest version is best illustrated by the people whose anger or fear seems to only have a 1 or a 10. There is no in between. What scientists are finding is that repeated, unresolved exposure to the fight, flight, or freeze system, without sufficient opportunity to recover, creates a hair trigger within our minds. We switch into aggression because that's what our environment has trained us to need.

The recovery part is hugely important because it seems to be the difference between someone who gains strength in the face of adversity and someone who is destroyed by it. Your muscles can serve as a good illustration. If you exercise regularly, with sufficient nutrients and rest between sessions, your muscles and overall fitness will improve. You will get stronger. But if you are eating the wrong foods, lacking sleep or time between exertion, your muscles will be prone to injury, your immune system will become frail, and you will crumble under the load.

In the same way, our brains have a system designed to keep us safe. It floods our body with strength and focus but afterward leaves us exhausted. If we experience a strong sense of fear, be it danger, rejection, or failure (the three big fears we all face), that system is engaged. If we recover and have the nutrition of meaningful relationships within which we can share those emotions and think them through, we can come out the other side stronger, more resilient. But if we are lacking relationships, we don't get the opportunity to process what has happened, and/or more stressful events take place before we're ready, we will be prone to injury and crumble under the load.

LOVE AND AUTHORITY

When I was a young teacher I also worked in campus ministry. We would reach out to students in an effort to start a new church that was born from the same style and message as the one I grew up in. In that season of my life, I spent a lot of time reading and listening to different versions of Christian teaching. One particular teacher was Dr. Greg Mitchell. He is a pastor in Vancouver, BC who had a memorable take on faith and psychology. He described God as being the embodiment of both perfect love and perfect authority. When we turn away from the ideals that he represents, we tend to turn away from one or the other of these major characteristics.

We turn from perfect love, Dr. Mitchell taught, by making up rules and faking our way toward looking good even though our hearts are dysfunctional. He called this religious obligation. Religions always have people who are there to earn their way into heaven by good deeds. So do political parties, charities, and any other form of civic engagement. Fundamental to this outlook is the protection of the ego. We show our worth to whatever deity or ideal to which we give honor. The problem is that at its core it is selfish. A selfish outlook is not perfect love. It can certainly suffice in a corrupt world, but there is a higher way.

We turn away from perfect authority and embrace rebellion and indulgence instead. Indulgence is different from enjoyment because you are using it to comfort yourself and numb the stress and pain of life. When you indulge, it's always with an internal negotiation about why you deserve it. That's to cover the shame you feel at breaking your own standard. The first person you rebel against is always yourself. You know what's right to do, you know the potential you have in you to be better than you are. That's why indulgence is so often secret, especially at first, though people who have lived in it often become more brazen over time. That internal lawyer starts winning against the standard you've set for yourself. Perhaps your standards aren't reasonable, though. Maybe you push yourself, and by extension your children, too far too fast. If perfect love and authority are the aim, that doesn't mean you will be perfect anytime soon.

God invites us into connection and even relationship with his divine perfection, but we embrace safer versions that let us be in control. We say "I must do this," or "I won't do that," instead of the relational statement, "I will do what's right." Religion or rebellion: though we all have one side of God we tend to lean toward, we end up getting caught on a pendulum. We spend time in rebellion, but we tire of it and decide to fix ourselves up. We form rules that we're determined to follow in order to make up for the shame we feel for our bad behavior. We follow our newly reformed religious model as long as we can bear it. Eventually we are exhausted, and we give in and swing back to rebellion and the eventual shame of failure that sends us back toward reform. Dr. Mitchell called it the pendulum swing.

As a 25-year-old, this rang true with me. In my own efforts to serve and please God as a minister and teacher, I was repeatedly thwarted by the corruption that my own heart and mind would produce. I wrestled with myself and the shame my own failures wrought in me. I was stuck on the pendulum between religious rules and rebellion, and seeing it clearly was some comfort, but renewing my thinking patterns was no simple journey.

Fast-forward 15 years. I was no longer in ministry but had been working steadily as a middle school teacher and then an elementary principal. My understanding of church had changed a great deal, but the idea of the pendulum had not left me. In fact, it had grown and developed in my mind. I was beginning to see the cycle more clearly and relating it to my work with kids. I was reading and listening to talks by Dr. Brene Brown about shame and blame, and it was filling in some missing pieces. I was watching kids grow from attention seekers into power strugglers. Then I realized that the pendulum idea and my power strugglers' mentality were one and the same. It all fit together. A power-struggler has two fundamental foes: themselves and others. Two sides to the pendulum.

I saw the pendulum in my reading about addiction cycles of shame and blame and heard about it from the school counselor and friends who worked in social work. I saw the struggle with self in a seminar about the disturbing rise of self-harm among teenagers. I saw my own struggles as a young man, when it had been about choosing to focus my effort on being someone good. That's not entirely true, though. It was more about avoiding being the bad person I felt that I was. What I lost in the process, and what eventually became my way out, was choosing good work. To protect your reputation and play it safe was to choose the way of struggle instead of creative, selfless risk. To choose good work, for its own sake, was more fulfilling. I wasn't proving anything. I was just doing good. Then I began to draw diagrams.

To struggle with yourself was a form of the same religious obligation I was turning to all those years ago. When I looked at the people around me, adults and children alike, I could see it more and more. I saw fearful parents whose sense of value as a mother or father was driving them to control and over-protect their growing children. Though people have non-religious versions, the idea was the same: a shame-driven, control-focused effort to improve yourself in order to cover up flaws and become some version of perfection that we wish we were. That can be new age yoga, clean eating, CrossFit, or political activism. Anyone chasing perfection is prone to the pendulum.

As I looked around me and read more and more, I saw the struggle with self more clearly. The thirst for value is driving people into perfectionism and rule-making. In order to feel better after your exhausting effort, you pursue selfish indulgences. To feel better after indulging, you need a new regimen; the old rules simply aren't enough. We need to find a new diet or a better system to organize our homes. We need new clothes and new cars and anything the sales departments tell us will make us better, more valuable. We compare ourselves to others and long for relief from the constant feeling that we're not good enough, we don't have what it takes, we've failed as parents and as people.

Our perfect rules are accompanied by an important set of polished behaviors that conceal and "fix" our self-loathing. We hate all our faults and therefore struggle to cover them up in hopes they'll go away. We sweep our fears and pain under the rug of our ever more distracted minds. But pain and fear will not be ignored, and our deeper selves come back to do battle with our perfect plans. They come back with a vengeance, and thus the pendulum swings.

Shame and blame are a cycle that every power struggler knows, and it's the simplest way you can tell when you're sinking into this mindset. It's driven by the crisis and comparisons that we all face. Make no mistake, we all have times when we fall into that cycle as well. As parents, we have times when we power struggle with our children, even as they do so with us. You would think our common struggle would help us relate to our children and them to us. But one of the biggest effects of self-focus is blindness to the needs of others.

If you think of the old-fashioned notion of pride, you might think of someone who thinks they're better than everyone else. Narcissists seem to get a lot of attention, ironically, but that's only half the picture. C.S. Lewis said it well when he wrote, "Humility is not thinking less of yourself, it's thinking of yourself less." It's important to understand that both sides of the power struggle are expressions of the same self-focused, prideful mentality. Pride doesn't say that you're the best at everything, it says you're the most important. Your strengths are more important than everyone else's strengths, but so too is your suffering and your weakness. Shame is just as prideful as blame. They both think that they are the most important, and they're both blind to the needs and motivations of others.

This is just as true in marriage. I can't tell you how many arguments I've had with my wife where I was completely convinced she was being selfishly unkind to me, and she was convinced of the exact same thing in return. I sit there waiting for her to stop being so focused on herself, blind to the fact that I was suffering from the same fault. Pride only sees pride in others. Selfishness only sees selfishness in others. And the only way out of it, besides sweeping it under the rug (to come back later as resentment and then contempt), is to shift your mind-set from power-struggling to something like problem-solving.

I have had many talks with a good friend who, along with her older sister, was sexually abused as a child. My friend expressed her own process of growing into adulthood plagued by overwhelming shame and an inward focus on her faults. For a time, she expressed her grief through perfectionism and escapist indulgence. At its worst, she wasn't able to function as a wife or a mother, and the shame only grew. If you had known her in that time, you would never have thought that she was prideful, but only depressed and introverted. After working through that pain, she found that she is neither of those things. Her personality shifted when she was able to deal with her pain.

Meanwhile, her sister expressed her grief by fighting against the world. She focused on the faults of others for her own suffering and externalized her pain into aggression and a powerful desire to be right. Her struggle expanded out as she grew up, from her parents, to her bosses, to a series of spouses. From an outside perspective, she did seem prideful. Though I don't know her well, her sister tells me of the same pain she struggled with from their childhood. Her pain, left unresolved, continues to sabotage her work and relationships.

As I mentioned in the last chapter, I've come to think of it as a swing set. Because of our personality, we may face one way, being inward or outward focused with our pain and comparisons. We lean on one side of the pendulum and kick away from the other. When I've talked with my friend about the abuse she's suffered, she concurred that even in her most painful and shame-filled moments, often in little ways known only to her, she would swing from shameful rulemaking to indulgence and blame. Her thirst for value became a need for control.

I know in my times of struggle, I've concealed my blame in an effort to look like I have it all together. I have also seen those who seem to have completely blocked out one side of the swing set. They have no shame. Perhaps they're concealing it as I was, but as I read about personality disorders and mental illness in light of the pendulum, and as I've seen the beginnings of some of those troubling thought patterns in the young children with whom I've worked, I wonder how bad the power struggle can get.

I have seen people who seem to have completely sealed off one side or the other of their pendulum. They seem to have built a wall next to their swing set, which, as you might imagine, makes for an uncomfortable and destructive life. If you've ever known someone stuck in the cycles of powerfully negative self-talk, abusive codependence, or narcissism, you know what I'm talking about. As with everyone who power struggles, it destroys their ability to do good work or relate to others.

CHAPTER 7

SEE YOUR IDEAL

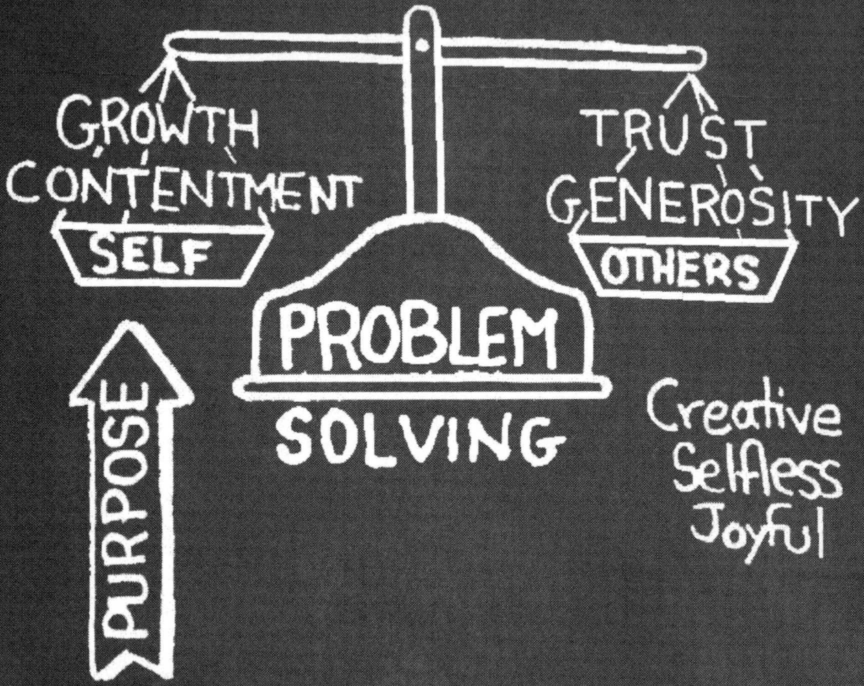
GROWTH
CONTENTMENT
SELF
TRUST
GENEROSITY
OTHERS
PROBLEM
SOLVING
PURPOSE
Creative
Selfless
Joyful

rene Brown, in her research about shame and vulnerability, describes people who are free from the pendulum as wholehearted. They believe they are worthy of love and affection; therefore they are able to receive both from the people in their lives. Carol Dweck's work on a growth versus fixed mind-set in children and adults describes the difference between success and failure as coming down to belief about whether your intelligence is malleable.

I am convinced that the lowest state of mind one can reach is that of the power struggler, and from there we need to find the highest mind-set. What is the aim toward which we not only want our kids to strive, but ourselves as well? This is huge. Without an aim, all you have to focus on is the negative. Telling your children, or yourself for that matter, not to think or act a certain way, still leaves you roaming. We need to aim at a specific target of success.

The mind-set of success is one where your question of value isn't necessarily answered. You can't just decide, as far as I can tell, to believe you're worthy of love. You can't just decide you're smart and then you will be. If that were true, then every kid who's been told they're smart for doing things they know are easy would never struggle with their worth. But the question of smartness, and in many ways value, is fundamentally a comparison. Comparison will suck the life out of you and others. The solution, the aim, is to set down the question of value and choose to move away from it.

Imagine, if you can, that you've put down the question of value. You don't wonder if you're a good mom or dad. You don't strive to be the greatest at work or worry if someone else gets the credit for your accomplishments. What I'm describing is the loss of ego that so many religious thinkers have striven for. What would it take, and what would you have to stop saying, and stop believing about yourself?

You also have to realize that your behavior and methods for motivating your kids is sending them toward or away from the same question of value. Think of the phrases you say when you're frustrated. Do you compare them to others? Do you ask them if they want others to think of them as one thing or another? Things like loser, bully, failure, mean. Those words can ring in their souls for a long time. Some of them—and you never know which ones—will stay with them long after you're dead. Perhaps those words will come out of their mouths one day when they're parents. Have you ever found yourself sounding like the angry parents you had? All the ways you've pushed your kids toward that same question of being great, of always measuring whether you're good or bad, those actions and statements are pushing them toward struggling for control when their value has run out.

The hard part is that many of the successful people you know are power struggling too. That's why comparison never works. It's easy to forget that the happiest people, the ones who are truly successful, are living out the values we know to be eternal. They don't struggle with who they are, so they don't run by ego or fret about their value. Sometimes this state of "happiness" can be very fleeting, and many people who've experienced it will chase it for the rest of their lives.

Mihaly Csikszentmihalyi wrote a bestselling and highly regarded book called *Flow*. In it, he wrote of the psychology of happiness and optimal performance and describes the state of mind of the most successful people in the world. In the place where your skills and your challenges are both at their peak, you will find yourself in a state of ecstasy, where your identity is lost and all you have before you is the work. This is called the flow state, or being "in the zone."

SELFLESS CREATIVITY

So our aim, the place where love and authority are perfected, is a place where our egos are set aside. We don't need to be talked up with self-esteem boosters, and we don't become focused on becoming the best or even just good enough. We aren't stuck thinking our smarts or our skills are unchangeable. Our ego, our shame, our worthiness, are all at rest. Failure stops being a threat because it's a sign of growth. Every failure is one step closer to the flow state. In such a state, our work becomes the goal and a joy all it's own. We're not anxious or controlling. We're not bored or needy. We are doing good for goodness sake.

The fruit of this problem-solving mind-set is that we can trust people. Their approval or rejection no longer touches the most tender places of value because the question of value is set aside. When people inevitably fail us, or even betray that trust, it doesn't shatter anything. These actions are just insights into their strengths and weaknesses. When we are wounded, we come to understand people better. In such a state, forgiving those who've hurt us, even loving our enemies, becomes almost easy.

In a study mentioned in the book *Drive*, by Daniel Pink, art critics looked at the quality of art. Some of the works were commissions that came with specific restrictions, while other artwork was created free of constraint. Without knowing which was which, the critics consistently found the commissioned works to be of lower creative and artistic quality. Pink argues that the difference was autonomy, and I don't think he's wrong, but there's also an important point to be made about approval. Making art for someone else to enjoy, and getting paid based on whether they approve, has a strong impact on our abilities. It changes our mind-set. When we tie ego back into the work we love, the quality of that work, and our enjoyment of it, will suffer. Real creativity is selfless. It's an outpouring of the problem-solving mind-set.

When I say creativity, I'm not only thinking of artistic endeavors. Wherever there are problems to be solved, and skills required to solve those problems, creativity is needed. In the same way, traditionally artistic activities are never free of conflict and resolution. Critical thinking and skillful execution are paramount to real art. Art is more than just expression, it's the skillful communication of an idea. All expression brings with it foundational ideas. If an artist doesn't know what those ideas are, then they're likely missing the point.

In my own experience as a teacher, there are two ways to get a struggling kid engaged in your classroom. One is to give them creative choices and ways to express themselves. The other is to give them a job to do that's legitimately helpful in class. Good work and creativity will always be elements of a healthy mind-set, and they also are simple tools to bring your child in crisis and comparison to a higher way of thinking.

A healthy mind-set will also be one of balance with self and others. Instead of struggling with yourself, you'll find contentment in the place in which you find yourself, your skills and strengths and level of discipline, even if it's not where you want to be. From that place of contentment, healthy growth will come.

Here's a little exercise to see if you understand what we're talking about, a little quiz perhaps. What's better, to try to be good, or to try to do good? When I ask people, about 90% inevitably answer that being good is the better target, as doing good will inevitably follow. I don't agree. I think that if you set your aim to be good, you're setting yourself as the center of your attention, and any good work that might fail, even if it is the better, more creative endeavor, will jeopardize your "goodness," and therefore you'll be less likely to try it.

YOU'RE NOT PERFECT

There is one last thing I'd like to say in describing the highest aim of our work as parents. To set our aim on perfection doesn't require us to be perfect, nor does it make you a hypocrite every time you fail. This is really important to remember. If you are constantly failing at anything, the outcome will be discouragement, resentment, and more failure. If you're always measuring yourself so you know where you stand, that's fine. But you can't expect perfection at any time in this process. You're getting closer. Your aim is growth.

Some people's reaction to repeated failure is to stop aiming for perfection. They settle for an easier path. The result of this is slippery, because like other forms of quitting, it's hard to stop once you've begun. The road back to a self-centered, power-struggling mentality is paved with comfort, so let me encourage you to keep perfect love and authority as your aim. Spend time thinking about what each of those qualities look like in the ideal. If your aim is defined by your weaknesses, then it's easy to lose track of your purpose. You become defined by yourself, and in the end you'll only be serving yourself.

The reality is that whether you aim for perfection or comfort, the result of life is still pain and suffering. If you're not currently failing as a parent, you'll sometimes fail as a spouse, or as a son or daughter. You'll have failures at work and in how you spend your money, not to mention that your health may fail no matter how vigilant you are. Your friends and family may betray you. There are all sorts of ways that life will be painful, and it will end in the death of everyone you know, if you do happen to live a long life. If you lose track of a purpose larger than yourself, then all that suffering is for nothing. Your purpose, the good work you set out to do, the ways that you make your community better than it would have been without you, these things make your suffering meaningful. There's no higher virtue than meaningful suffering.

If you let aimlessness and selfish comfort take hold, it doesn't take a lot of suffering before you become filled with nihilistic resentment. That resentment and vengefulness can bring you to the brink of destruction. In my line of work, I see that destruction when I work with the hardest kids. I have seen the seeds of resentment growing, and I have watched where they lead. As a teacher and principal, I have also read about the minds of school shooters. They are just the extreme examples of the same thought process. Kids suffer. They fail often and they inflict pain on each other. It's unavoidable. Some kids are less than successful on average, and if their aim is their own comfort and value, then their failures very quickly become someone else's fault. That fault spreads, sometimes to the whole world.

Meaningless pain requires blame. For every victim there is a villian, as every hero movie and children's story tells them, and they go looking for someone to take the blame for their pain and failure. At first, and this is a very satisfying outlook, their pain is the fault of whatever person has mocked or laughed at them. There's always one, but it doesn't stop there. Soon the people around are at fault, for they should have protected the person. Then the teachers and principal, the parents and neighbors, should have all helped and cared, but they didn't. Then the system as a whole is to blame. Governments perhaps, or people of other religions or cultures. Taken to its end, all these people must be made to pay and in the most painful way possible. And who would you hurt if you wanted to show your vengeance upon the world except the people most prized and protected when you never were.

It's a dark road, and few take it to its end, but we've all stepped on that path. I remember trying to explain to a young teacher how a parent could bring their child to live with someone they knew was sexually abusive. How could a mother bring her daughters into an environment where she knew they would suffer so horribly? There are lots of reasons, perhaps, but here's how I said it: Think of how you feel when you're mad at your spouse. You don't care about how they're feeling because they should be caring about you right now. Don't they know what they've done? Now imagine that you never let that feeling go. It fades, surely, but you don't resolve the issue and it festers over time, and the next time your feelings are hurt, it all comes rushing back. Your anger and sadness turn bitter.

Now imagine that you aim that at your children. That you begin to resent them in the same way. Their suffering is an inconvenience to you. And even if you're not going to take out your vengeance on them, perhaps you won't be quite so vigilant in protecting them as you might have been. Perhaps if they do get hurt, it's their own fault anyway. Otherwise, how will they learn? As a principal, I have heard all these reasons before.

So keep your aim set high, and find the good work that is right in front of you. Don't try to bear the weight of the world, but lift heavy things that you didn't realize you were strong enough to carry. Lift the weight of your parents' failures by failing less. Lift the burden of your neighbor kids who need a loving home to visit where perfect love and authority are the aim. As you do, not only will you get stronger, but you'll learn to put down, and maybe even walk away from, your own question of value.

CHAPTER 8

BUILD A LADDER: GENUINE AFFECTION

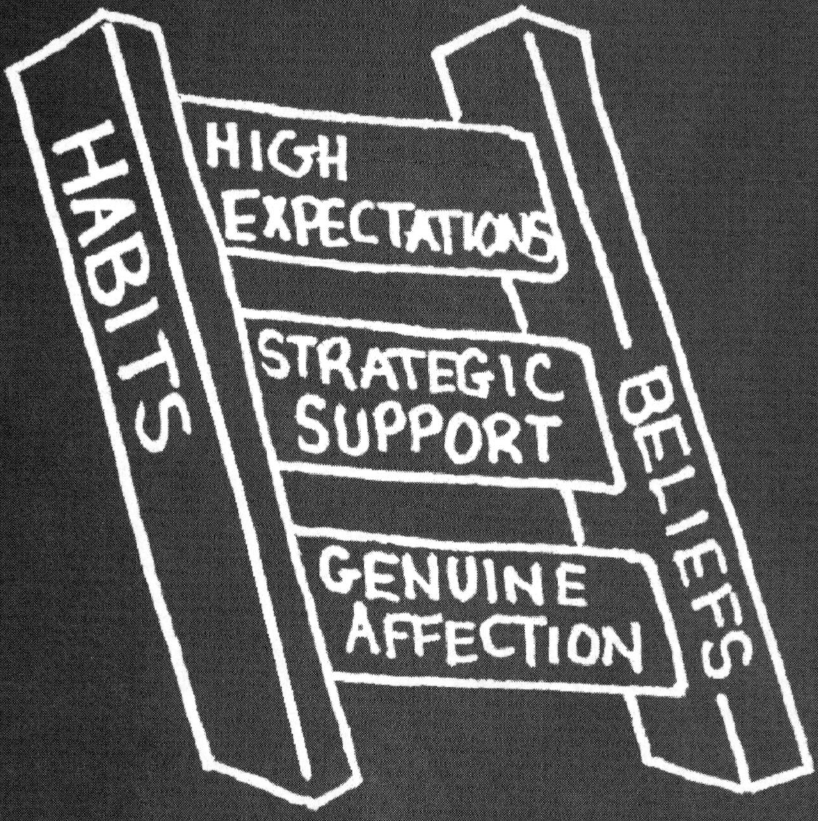
HABITS
HIGH EXPECTATIONS
STRATEGIC SUPPORT
GENUINE AFFECTION
BELIEFS

t's time to learn to help our kids climb out of the negative mentality they're stuck in. Whether they're searching for attention and value with needy, impulsive selfishness, or struggling for control of themselves or others in a destructive pendulum, we are the ladder they need. In the coming chapters, we're going to explore how to build that ladder, starting with the first rung: genuine affection. We'll look at each step of support you can offer your kids, and the habits and beliefs you need to address along the way.

Before we do that, we need to mention the ground upon which your ladder will set: staying calm. Your emotional state sets the tone for how your kids will respond to the world, and that includes how they'll respond to you. You can't expect them to control their impulsive, needy reactions if you can't do the same. Let me explain.

If we're going to dismantle the web of shame and blame that's captured our children and sunk them into a cycle of struggling with themselves and others, then we have to start with shame. Shame isn't a feeling, it's a deeply seated belief we hold that tells us that we're not worthy of love and belonging. Regardless of our upbringing, we all have this lie set deep within us. There's a reason that the most prolific story of creation told around the world is all about shame, hiding, covering, and blaming. This is universal.

Even though shame (thinking you're worthless) is often confused with guilt (thinking you've done something bad), they couldn't be more different. Shame tells you that you have no value, no matter how many good things you may have done. Guilt says you did something bad and you need to fix it. Shame drives a little war inside you as your heart longs to feel worthy, but it won't let you believe it. Guilt says it's your fault and therefore you should fix it. Shame takes every bad thing you've done, whether it's your fault or not, and says you deserved it, it is more evidence that you're worthless, and you're useless too. Guilt is good because it will call you to action and empower you to make yourself better. Shame beats you down and tells you there's no point in trying, while simultaneously driving you to work at a tireless pace.

Where guilt is so powerful is when kids feel guilty in the face of their errors, it actually blocks the shame. According to University of Houston research professor Dr. Brene Brown, whose focus is on shame and vulnerability, young kids who describe experiencing guilt when they make mistakes, instead of shame, are far more likely to be successful in school and less likely to participate in risky behaviors with sex, drugs, and alcohol. If we can change the pattern of thinking, we can change the direction of their lives.

The bottom line is that shame is driven by our question of value. If our aim is for our kids to put down that question, then guilt can be a great tool to help get them there. What guilt says is that you did something wrong. It's your fault. What's fantastic about this is that admitting your guilt gives you power. If you are at fault, you can improve your situation. You aren't helpless to your circumstances or the feelings of others. Guilt is the opposite of victimhood. I can't tell you how many conversations I've had with kids about their choices that pivots on their guilt and making a plan to improve their relationships with others.

The result of guilt-focused correction is that you can problem solve the situation without breaking relationship. When you focus on guilt and solving the problem, you're not focusing on shame and anger and resentment. As a parent, it requires that you control your own anger and frustration and avoid putting it on your kids. That's easier said than done, and those habits and beliefs that you've already established in your parenting are just as hard to change in yourself as they are in your kids. Staying calm is the foundation of effective discipline.

It's time to stand in your own guilt, rather than the shame cycle you've been stuck in as a parent. As you do this more (don't make this an all or nothing situation), then your kids can start to look to the future with hope rather than shame. They can learn from their mistakes, rather than believe that they're always like this, or they're just like their father, or some other version of being resigned to the fact that bad things will happen again because that's who they are. Help them to put down the shame and let guilt empower your parenting and your children. Stay calm.

Your most powerful weapon as a parent or a teacher, when it comes to dealing with the shame kids are struggling with, is first displaying genuine affection. If you want to hold them to a high standard, you have to first communicate that you care about them. That's different than wanting them to like you. I've seen that trap with parents and teachers alike: wanting to be the friendly older sibling to your kids. Not only is that selfishly trying to avoid necessary conflict, and your kids know it and lose respect for you, but it's not what they need. Your kids have friends and teachers, but they only have one mom and one dad. They need someone who will be like a wall that holds up the protective ceiling that keeps the storms at bay. All that begins with a genuine display of affection for the person they are right now, including their weaknesses and mistakes.

This is harder than it sounds, especially if you are in the throws of an angsty teenager who takes everything personally and wants to power struggle with you day after day. That can build up a lot of resentment, which gets communicated in the tone of voice you use. Kids hear your frustrated tone in response to something they think isn't a big deal, and they interpret it to mean that you don't care about them. They're not entirely wrong. If your frustration is that they need to change in order for you to stop resenting them (i.e., forgive them), you're loving some version of your child that doesn't exist. Genuine affection means you want them around to actually do stuff together.

When you're at your best as a parent, you see where they are, with all their struggles and fighting, and you look for a way through it. It doesn't offend you that they are where they are. It just is. On your best day, you even begin to see the way through the pain and anguish you're feeling, so you can just be with them. Remember the flow state we mentioned in the last chapter? What if you could get into that state as a parent: a place of selfless, creative purpose where your skills and the challenges you face are enough to make you put down your own question of value.

Sometimes we feel unloved by our kids because of the effort they aren't giving. When we allow that feeling to control us, it will interfere with our ability to parent. Often the first thing that comes out of their mouths is, "What's the big deal?" but that's not what they mean. What they're actually saying is, "Why is this bad habit of mine that you've allowed to continue for years by fixing things for me and ignoring my disobedience suddenly making you mad?" Every time you're frustrated with them for their socks or their homework, or whatever, they may be hearing it as, "I wish you were someone else." If you're not careful, your frustration can strike their heart more than their mind, and it fuels the fire of shame that says even your parents don't like you.

Again, remember that frustration gets in the way of being an effective parent. When you are frustrated, your kids feel rejected because you're not satisfied with what they think is their best effort. Rejection is shame fuel, and sends them toward the power struggle, so you've got to tone it down. It's time to raise the bar for your own resiliency, and stop seeing your kids' behavior, good or bad, as the way you're going to feel good about yourself. It's not their job to make you feel valuable.

All frustration is, is your own expectations getting in the way of a calm version of you. If you're frustrated that they keep making the same mistake over and over, you need to realize that they aren't doing it on purpose. It isn't personal. They lack the skills to do a good job. And whose job was it to teach them those skills anyway? Yours, of course. So settle down with your anger, lower your expectations, make the steps to success shorter, give them more time to do the same task, do all the things you need to do to help them stop failing so much. You'll both feel better in the end.

How much of your frustration with your kids is coming from your own question of value? (Don't they even love me? Am I a terrible mother?) Whenever you look to your kids to get your emotional needs met, they will receive it as shame. They will think you're just using them to feel good about yourself and that you don't actually like them as a person. I've seen kids as young as five give a look to adults that says, "What is your problem?" Even when they can't describe it, they feel it. They believe that you're using them for your own gratification. They believe they aren't worth anything to you unless they're someone else, someone more perfect. Maybe they're not wrong.

What if you could show calm, direct affection in the face of disappointment? What if your own feeling of being loved or valuable could be completely taken out of the picture so you could see the steps they need to take to get to the level they need to be? You can do it with other people's kids (sometimes). It's time to take the bad emotional habits you've formed with your family and build new ones.

I've tried with many kids to make a list of things they're thankful for as a remedy to the power struggling they face every day. I haven't had a lot of success. When a kid's focus is negative, it's hard for them to emotionally invest in someone saying they are lucky compared to kids in Africa who are starving. They feel like they're starving too. But if you can corral the negativity toward a specific time and place where they could have done something differently to make the situation better instead of worse, then there's opportunity and hope for next time. That's the guilt we were talking about earlier. Guilt is better than shame.

SECRET SHAME IS
ALWAYS MORE POWERFUL

For some people, their shame is well hidden. They seem to be on the offensive, though, when it comes to their mistakes and the problems life brings. They are repeatedly portraying themselves as the victim in different circumstances. In time, it becomes a habit that must be broken to get at the shame underneath which is the source of their failure. I say failure because if you can't see your own fault in life, even if that fault is only part of the story, then you can't grow and learn from what's going on around you.

You might only see this once in a while with some people. Shame can be focused on one relationship or situation. We've all been around people who make us feel inferior just by their presence. The same can happen in certain settings where your weaknesses are acutely felt. Even if it's not chronic and widespread, it still is worth addressing each time it arises. Reactive blame, especially if combined with anger and public posturing, is a sure sign that shame is sitting underneath.

As a principal, I can't tell you how many times the teachers, staff, or I have become the reflexive target of parents, students, or each other. For example, when a kid's feelings are hurt, or there's some kind of conflict, I've had parents furious that the school wasn't doing something about it, even when no one knew about it until now. The kids had not told anyone about it, but we should have known. It didn't matter that both kids were at fault.

For educators, the only way through this attack is not to take it personally. For that parent, blaming is a habit, and they almost certainly do it in every other relationship they're in. Of course, sometimes we are at fault, and apologizing where you can is fundamental to every healthy relationship. What we're trying to avoid is our kids learning the same habits. This style of conflict undermines every relationship in which it's used, even though it feels good to declare and demand that others are at fault. It feels good to get others to bow to our righteous anger, and it eventually gets aimed at everyone.

BUILD YOUR LADDER

Before you can resolve the problems created by shame and blame, you have to establish genuine affection. It's fundamental. When it comes to your own kids, perhaps you think this will come easily. You know you love them, and when you ask them, they say they know that too. But keep in mind two things. One, they will always say that, even if they don't believe it; and two, you will always tell yourself that, even if you don't believe it.

If you've been in conflict with your kids for the same attitude or misbehavior for months or years, resentment is a real thing that can seep into any relationship. Telling yourself it isn't there doesn't do a thing to help it. You have to stop and ask yourself why you get frustrated so easily with your kids. Why do certain moments set you off in a flash with a frustration that's out of proportion to the matter at hand? You often can't see your own resentment, but you've probably observed it in others. How many times have you watched others parenting their kids with a edge of harshness and thought they were overreacting? Well, you fall into the same issue when they're watching you.

Every time you respond to your kids' behavior with frustration, you run the risk of breaking the first rung of the ladder. If your kids don't believe in your genuine affection, then you've made it impossible to hold them to a high standard or support them in their success. They may obey you in the moment, but if they don't believe you care about them, they will reject you in the long run. That's a high cost to pay for obedience, and it will work against the long-term goal of parenting: to teach, and to have a healthy relationship that lasts into adulthood.

One question you need to ask yourself is how much your own wounds as a living human being are affecting your parenting. Are you still hurting from the things others have said and done to you, and is that pain getting aimed at your children? People in power struggles with themselves will always get in them with others. People who are trying to prove they're good enough will hurt others by demanding they prove it too. Power struggle is a two-way street, so the fact that you're battling your children means you're battling within. We all are, but we can't escape the effects of shame without shining light on it.

That's not to say that parents don't correct their children on a regular basis, but that correction is all fit within the context of affectionate relationship. If you have multiple kids, you also have to gauge how you're doing with each child. Your relationship with each of your children will be so different, and when one kid is by your side and connected to your passions and direction, the other might be distant and isolated. Your job as a parent is not to give them all the same attention. Your job is to give them what they need. If that means spending way more bedtimes nose to nose with one child than the other, then do it. Build and support your children where they are.

Remember that every person is on the spectrum between power struggling and problem solving. If you can catch their question of value before it descends into comparison and chaos, then you've rescued them from a world of hurt. Sometimes kids (and grownups), have battles they're facing that you know nothing about. Be the responsive adult who maintains interest without making it about you. Stand nearby and at the ready to hear what's bothering them.

Prepare yourself for the fact that from your perspective, their struggles may sound trivial. They're mad at their sister for getting away with everything, but of course that's one-sided. Remember that it doesn't matter what the issue is, your first goal is to give their emotions validity, even if their perspective is flawed. You can deal with that later. The first rung of the ladder is affection. There's something in what they're sharing that you can give respect and honor to. Tell them you're proud of how they're handling a tough situation with honesty, not hiding their feelings or stuffing them down. They're being open, and that's how loving relationships are maintained.

Sitting with your son or daughter in their pain is the foundation for your own ability to be candid with them. When you've honored their thoughts and feelings about something, and they've really heard it and received it, then you've got a 30-second window to say something that brings them back to reality. What will you say in that moment? What is the thought process that we can use to replace their defensive blame?

Because blame is one of the defense mechanisms to hide and protect our shame from the view of others, we have to tackle both shame and blame at once. As I've mentioned, a great replacement for blame is guilt. Is the other person responsible for the problem? How much did you make it worse or better? Let's face the facts together. From there, I think there's a conversation to be had that gets into the shame too. Can you find a larger perspective about the suffering of others? Can you think about the pain that other people have experienced that might make you thankful for your own circumstances? Thankfulness goes a long way toward bringing you into contentment.

DON'T APPEASE, DON'T IGNORE

There's an old adage for new teachers that says, "Don't smile until Christmas." I have given that advice many times, and I've used it each time I was new to a job or school. You have to set the tone of authority first, then you can be their friend. For parents it is the same. Your love for them has to first be connected to authority. You have to be able to establish your will in order to then give your kids the meaningful choices they crave.

If you give kids what they want right away, they may get the impression that you're giving in to their demands. Maybe it's because you either aren't willing, or aren't able, to stand up against those demands. You're avoiding the conflict. If you're willing to give your children something they don't need or shouldn't have in order to avoid their manipulation, and all the stress that comes with it, you're no longer in it for them. You are being self-centered and too weak to love them in their state of immaturity. And they know it. In order to make freedom and choice a genuine gift to them, it has to be based on what you believe is best for them. That means you have to be willing and able to stand up to them and tell them no when you genuinely think it's best. It also means that you can't just tell them no all the time because you're tired or a bit resentful that they interrupt you and need things all the time.

Being strong enough to tell children no (and mean it), besides having their best in mind, means you can handle what life is going to throw at them. They're just kids, and they aren't tough enough to handle life, so they look to adults to see what they should be afraid of, what they should find disgusting, and who they should trust or dislike. But if that adult can't even overcome a child's strong will, how will they be tough enough to protect them from the world? I have seen many classrooms descend into chaos because the adult couldn't stand up to the mean kid. The adult would tell them to stop, threaten punishment, sound angry, but it was all a show. They would walk away and say the real punishment was coming "next time." But next time never comes.

Your kids will get the same message from you when you give in to their selfish, manipulative demands. If a seven-year-old can defeat you in a battle of wills, who is going to protect that kid from the bully or the mean teacher or the unfair policy? These are almost always the same families who come into the school screaming about how unjust things are, and then disappear for the rest of the year. They are trying to show their kid that they love them and that they're willing to stick up for them. They might say that family comes first, but they can't actually handle the conflict that is required to see real change come about. They use the same tactic with their children: ignore the problem, yell about it, then ignore it again.

On some level, you have to appreciate the conflict that parenting requires. Every time that you hurt your child's feelings, if done for their good, you are working to reset their selfish worldview and help them rightly see their place in the world. When you ignore the problem and then explode in frustration, you are making them more insecure, more needy and impulsive, and eventually they will start to dominate you in order to find the safety that you can't provide.

There's a reason why it takes two people who are very different from each other to make a baby. Research shows us that it also takes two to raise them. In the best circumstances, those same differences will serve to bring balance of both warmth and firmness. When parents set their aim on perfect love and perfect authority, they are giving their children what they need. Not only that, but we each need to cultivate both sides of our own personality, growing stronger if we tend to side with affection, and being more tender and understanding if we tend toward authority.

If we are going to be the ladder on which our children can climb into a healthy mentality, our kids need genuine affection from us. We need to stay calm and control our own impulses, seek to understand their struggles, look for bad habits to which we can provide consistent feedback, and break down wrong thinking and unhealthy beliefs they've taken on about themselves and others. That requires that we be loving and strong.

CHAPTER 9

STRATEGIC SUPPORT

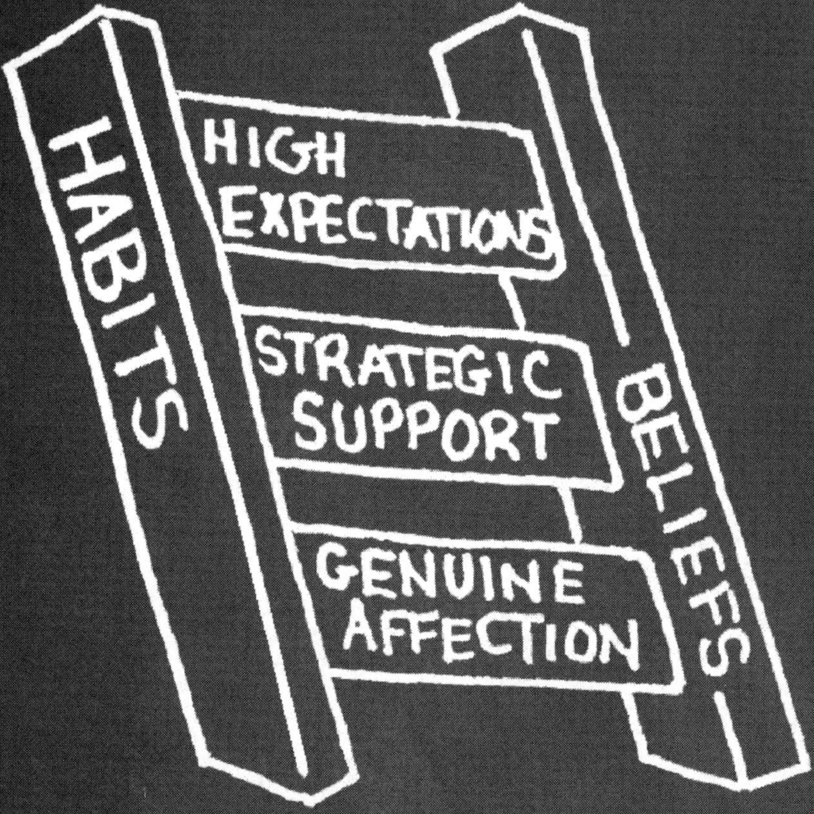
HABITS
HIGH EXPECTATIONS
STRATEGIC SUPPORT
GENUINE AFFECTION
BELIEFS

You've established your care for your child, meaning that you're willing to make loving demands of them regardless of their emotional outbursts and resistance. You genuinely care for their struggles, and you recognize their efforts and are responsive to their pain. Now it's time to help them grow up. We need to stop letting them fail at the same things again and again. We need to avoid the power struggle that will inevitably come with time, we need to teach them to navigate conflict and fight fair in a loving relationship, and we need to look where they trip instead of where they fall. It's time to give our kids the strategic support they need to be successful.

First, we need to realize that the defiance, power struggles, and emotional outbursts that you're dealing with as a parent are actually failures. Your kids are failing, you and they both know it, and they need your help. Right now you might be feeling the weight of such a statement as a judgment upon your skill as a parent, or you may feel the guilt that comes with realizing that you haven't done all you could have done in the early years. Remember that your question of value, about parenting or anything else, is only going to get in the way. Put that down and let's get to work.

The first thing to do is make a list of the times and topics that are really tripping your kids up. Is it when you're all piled up at the front door getting ready to go somewhere? Is it at bedtime when they suddenly become the world's most ruthless negotiator, demanding five more minutes and a gallon of water to be consumed in 2-ounce increments? Whatever the setting, it's about time that you open your eyes to what is tripping them up. Don't say it's everywhere, because that won't help. What's the worst moment for you? Pick your battle and prepare to fight it for their sake.

MAKE "MISTEAKS"

Having been a math teacher, it was hard to get to kids' hearts in the course of a normal day. I knew that kids needed more wisdom and steady guidance than they were getting from the onslaught of negative media they were being exposed to, so I had to find a way. What I wanted to be, and as a principal I've worked toward the same goal, was the voice of calm reason that would counteract the selfish messages that they were receiving.

Each week, when I was teaching middle school, I used to put a proverb from different countries on the board. One of the things mathematics has always taught me is that the universe speaks the same language. What works in the hearts of people in ancient Africa will also work in Peru, or in an ultra-modern United States. There's no lie that hasn't been told before and no truth that can't be rightly applied to a child in any classroom. One such proverb went like this, "Make misteaks." I thought it was funny so I put it on a big bulletin board in my class. It was even funnier when the students began to tell me that they didn't get it. How ironic that they didn't know how to spell "mistakes."

Another memorable proverb, supposedly Chinese in origin, went something like this, "Do not look where you fell, but where you slipped." As with most such statements, it served mostly to confuse the kids who read it. But to me it was a reminder to be a better teacher. I needed to take responsibility for finding the places my students were repeatedly slipping up and make the steps smaller, the supports more accessible, and the practice more relevant and practical. It was my job to make sure they could find the success that builds real confidence.

When I graded a test or assignment, I would sometimes find that most of the kids had failed. I was tempted to blame them for the failure and give them a bunch of makeup work and hoops through which to jump if they wanted to keep their grades up. This was the same system I was raised in. It was their responsibility to be ready for the test after all. The inevitable result was that a group of kids began to give up on being successful in school. I had to learn to be generous with my support and go to where the kids were, not where I arbitrarily decided they "should" be. A colleague at that time taught me that kind people don't "should" on one another. It's good advice for parents too.

As a parent, I have fallen for the trap of should many times. "I told them to clean their room. Now they get what they deserve." True enough, but if we all got what we deserve, none of us would fare very well. What I've learned as a parent and educator is that I have to look where people are slipping and build the supports they need. If they are failing at bedtime, then I need to start earlier, make the steps more manageable, make my expectations clearer, my voice more calm. You can't say you've taught something if your students haven't learned it. That just means you told them. You can't say you've raised your kids if they're not succeeding in their life. It's time to really teach them. It's time to give them the strategic support they need.

Q-TIP

In my role as principal, I go every other year to get retrained on when and how to take hold of kids. There are very few children at my school who are trying to hurt themselves or others in a way that they can't control, but when they need you to intervene, it's vital that you be prepared. It's the least fun part of my job, and over my years in education it seems to be increasing in severity and frequency. In fact, part of the process of developing this book was inspired by the clear rise of kids coming to our school with such dramatic and violent outbursts.

One of the most helpful parts of what's called Crisis Prevention Institute (CPI) training, and I've taken it several times now, is the little acronym Q-TIP: Quit Taking It Personal. A student's (or your child's) inability to handle school, and their angry efforts to gain control of their world, aren't really about you. They are feeling overwhelmed and underprepared. It's not personal; they literally cannot handle their life. They are missing the skills and strength they need to cope with their challenges. Of course they should have them, and yes it's sad that they don't, but it's also full of hope that you can help them learn skills and gain strength if you can go through these struggles with them.

As a middle school teacher, I also had to remember not to take things personally. Teaching middle school takes a special kind of person. If elementary teachers are motherly and high school teachers all wish they were coaches or college professors, then middle school teachers are the quirky inbetweeners. That's not much different than the kids themselves, and in my years there I learned a few lessons about handling the terrible things kids say.

Middle school is the phase when kids learn their words have power. They trade vicious insults with friends and enemies alike. The old saying that "power corrupts" is certainly true when I taught middle school. I was used to private-school juniors and seniors, and I had no idea how to handle kids saying horrible things to each other all the time. Not only that, I needed to learn how to avoid the power struggle that inspires those horrible statements. In my first year, I was regularly disturbed by the things my students would say to me and each other. I would get offended and impatient to the point of yelling at them, but my anger rarely worked for more than a few minutes, and then the kids were at it again.

One day in that first year, my wife and I went to spend the weekend at my in-laws' house. I thought I would find some much-needed sympathy, since they were both veteran teachers. I got none. Instead, my father-in-law lovingly rebuked the low expectations I had for myself as a teacher. "Yelling is not okay. You really need to stop it." He may not have said it just that straightforwardly, but that's what I heard. I took it in but didn't have much of an answer. Perhaps I needed to rethink my strategy rather than blame the kids. The kids certainly weren't going to change, so if I expected improvement, it would have to come from me.

This took me aback, and I retreated to think it over. I soon found myself next to my mother-in-law, who had some advice of her own. She had worked for years as a substitute in her nearby community grade school. She was much loved by the kids who saw her year after year in their classrooms. She had a trick or two on how to establish authority without the power struggle, and I was all ears.

She told me how she would get out a post-it notepad and tell the kids she was writing the names of all the kids who weren't listening. If their names were written twice before recess, then they would owe five minutes. But she would never tell kids if their names were written down or not. They were always guessing, and therefore always trying to make sure their names didn't get on there twice. I was amazed the first time I tried it as the normally chatty kids were whispering to each other that I was writing on the pad. It didn't require the public shaming and inevitable giving up (power struggle) as writing names on the board did. This was the beginning of my first major breakthrough about supporting kids and avoiding the power struggle. Get out of the way.

TRIANGULATE

I now call it triangulating: separate yourself from the rules, rewards, and consequences. Don't make the punishment come from you, but set it up as the third point of a triangle. This way you don't feed into the story they tell themselves about how you don't like them, or you aren't fair. If you establish the system of punishment ahead of time, then stand next to them to look at it and help them navigate that system, you're suddenly their ally and not their enemy. You become the beloved coach who helps them win and improve, rather than the hated referee who never makes the right call.

Eventually, as a teacher, it dawned on me that middle schoolers don't actually know what they are saying. They are trying out different ways to feel their power and push the boundaries of what their words can do to people. At the same time, they were all well-versed in the need to be completely impervious to one another's statements. As an adult, if my friend or coworker was to insult me like this, I might not be angry, but I would certainly think they were completely unskilled at friendship or social interactions. For these kids, it was a missing skill, and as a teacher, it's my job to give them skills. In my last year as a middle school teacher, I was tested in how well I could avoid the power struggle. In the process, I also started to see how to overcome it.

I was standing in the hallway between classes, keeping an eye on the mayhem, and the kids were mingled outside the door of the class next to mine. Among them was an eighth grader named Ben who was in my class when he was just starting out in middle school two years before. He was with a couple girls, and I looked over to smile in their direction when he shouted, "Mr. Z, that tie you're wearing is stupid looking."

He was taking a shot at me, and I knew it was all a show for the audience around him. In that moment, I felt my pulse flare up. This was a cool tie. I got it at Goodwill. I thought of going after him, ridiculing him back, or ignoring him and rising above it. But then the better part of me stepped in, "I really like you, Ben." I said and smiled warmly at him. I looked him right in the eyes and he rolled his eyes and smiled back as the girls on both sides of him gave a little giggle.

The next day, at the same passing period, we were all back in the same spots like it was a play that we had rehearsed the day before. Immediately Ben said his line, "Mr. Z, your shirt is ugly." He squinted a bit and set his jaw.

I smiled up at him, right on cue. "I love you, Ben." I said. He rolled his eyes again, with a bigger smile this time. The girls laughed even louder as they walked away.

The next day, we were all in our places once more. Right on cue, "Your shirt is stupid, Mr. Z" he smirked, now only half-heartedly trying to insult me.

"I love you, Ben." I replied. He smiled back at me. The girls laughed once more. And that was that. He never bothered me again. Not only that, but I later learned from his teachers that his eighth grade year had been a turning point for him. He had come into his own and given up the power struggling that he had become known for in years prior. I like to think I helped that along, not just by avoiding the power struggle, but by defeating it with genuine affection and strategic support.

WE NEED CONFLICT

The bottom line is that kids don't know how to fight well. Our relationships in general, and our parenting style as an extension, have gotten so averse to conflict and hurt feelings that we've left our kids completely incapable of resolving conflict in a healthy way. Conflict resolution is a requirement far more than algebra, and yet parents will die on the hill of good grades and going to college far more than they'll emphasize real social skills. Facing intensely complex relationships equipped only with the phrase, "be nice," is like trying to build a house with only a hammer. Of course be nice, but that's not enough in a world of power strugglers and attention seekers.

So often parents and teachers land on two unhelpful sides of how to deal with conflict: avoid it and appease it. The appeasers want to make sure everyone is nice all the time in order to protect kids from having fear or sadness. In kids' movies, people go on and on about how kindness works, but it won't help when your children face off with kids who are dysfunctional and abusive. The thought is that everyone's kindness will be enough to transform them, but on a peer level that simply doesn't work. Without getting too deep into the topic, this mentality is a big part of what makes some people more susceptible to PTSD. Their rose-colored glasses won't prepare them for people who are genuinely malicious.

These parents and teachers are the rescuers. Whenever something goes wrong among the kids, the answer is that kids should have come and got an adult. How will they learn to solve their problems if the grownups are always doing it for them? How will rude kids learn that no one wants to be friends with jerks, if they don't taste a little exclusion as a consequence? We need to equip kids to resolve conflict with calm words and strong principles. As C.S. Lewis wrote in his children's book *The Last Battle*, "Courteous words or else hard knocks are [a warrior's] only language." Train kids to stand up to their peers (and not give in to manipulation), and all their future relationships will be improved.

There are many well-intentioned efforts to avoid conflict among kids partly inspired by the astonishing growth of suicide among adolescents, especially middle schoolers. But what research shows on the subject is that the number of kids reporting that they've been the victims of abuse has actually gone down as the suicide rate has doubled among middle schoolers in the last decade. Fewer kids are being mistreated, but the effect is worse. It's not entirely clear why, but it seems that the creation of open venues (the internet), where insults and mockery are inescapable, plays a significant part. If kids could simply go home from school to escape a tormenter, that person can now continue into the evening hours. Where an insult might have been heard by classmates and passed around by word of mouth, those insults are now available for hundreds to see, and passed around digitally for weeks.

The other side of the problem is the parent who leaves kids to work it out themselves. Having no skills to resolve conflict, and being a kid, almost always results in some version of might makes right. The oldest child is not only strongest, but they're better at arguing, convincing others, getting their way. When you leave siblings or friends to fix problems without support, it doesn't take long before the older kids become the refs and the winners of every game. The kids below them often develop a chip on their shoulders, especially if they have a competitive side to them. That sense of entitlement is incredibly hard to break when they start dishing out the treatment they received at the hands of the kids above them. This is where terrible hazing rituals come from. Ignoring the problem makes it worse, just as appeasing and rescuing do. The only way to teach kids to endure and navigate conflict is through actual conflict. The only way to keep from making their world a pecking order full of perpetual frustration is for you the adult to be the coach.

RULES FOR FIGHTING

The threat of peer torment is very real, but we mustn't forget that avoiding heavy objects will leave us weak. Emotional weakness is at epidemic proportions. We need to help our children gain emotional muscle by giving them the heavy weights that are at their limits, but not past. Just like exercise, there are techniques to learn in order to avoid injury. If we're going to train kids in healthy relational conflict, it helps to have some rules. Do's and Don'ts.

As a school leader, conflict is a daily part of what I do. Kids are constantly in conflict with each other, and it is difficult to teach kids when they arrive in my office angry and hurting. The actual lesson has to be taught in the midst of, not by avoiding crisis. That only happens by creating a set of lessons and phrases that we can lean back on in those times of stress. If you create a common language of problem solving, it will serve you well when everyone is worked up. At our school, it's the 7 Habits of Happy Kids material inspired by the famous book by Sean and Stephen Covey. Simple, principled phrases are a great resource in stressful circumstances, and it's fantastic to hear kids using those phrases to navigate stressful decisions on their own.

There are kids in every school who are most likely to be involved in conflict, and very often they have been part of some serious struggles at home from an early age. They start out needy and push against the rules with fidgety and impulsive fear of rejection and failure. They need constant affirmation, and we as educators try to give it to them in the midst of all the other things teachers and staff have to accomplish. If we can't get through to them, they end up pushing back harder and harder as they grow, eventually fighting everyone around them. At the foundation of that pushback are two destructive beliefs I have heard countless kids express in their anger and conflict: blaming others for every failure and assuming ill intent.

Blame says it's all someone else's fault. I'm the victim here, and if any of this problem is my fault, it is so small it's not worth mentioning. That belief can grow into a full-blown victim narrative, and it is a disturbingly common symptom among kids. That belief is often at the heart of their lying (they all lie, by the way), and it is an effective story we can tell ourselves when the shame that follows failure threatens to overwhelm us. Adults aren't exempt from this trap either. I've talked to more than one manager, in all sorts of fields, who battles with the victim mentality in their employees. It will not only destroy your relationships, but it will defeat any purposeful work you try to engage in.

The second belief is assuming ill intent: the wrong belief that others are out to hurt us. If blame makes us the hero of our story, then the ill intent of others makes them the villain and our anger completely justified. We all love to assume the intentions of others, declaring that we can look into their soul when they make a mistake or wrong us. "I did it on accident," we say, "but they did it on purpose." People fall into the routine of using this story wherever they go. We need to change their routine.

We all enjoy feeling like a martyr once in a while, but it takes time to build a narrative that you take with you into your work and your relationships. The difference, I think, is that some of us have people in our lives willing to interrupt our selfish thinking. As parents, that's our first job: to engage in the conflict our kids need. Don't avoid this one. Don't "choose your battles" here. There is so much on the line, and we need to change their routine.

I'm convinced that our collective thirst for hero stories in movies and media is fueled by our cultural hunger to paint our enemies as evil and inhuman. There's nothing wrong with these stories, but it's remarkable that we are so saturated in them. These stories make it easy to justify destroying our enemies. Real life is never so simple, and even the most evil people in the world still tell themselves that they were just protecting their family or taking what they deserved. This struck me most powerfully when hearing a veteran talk about how the Taliban loves Star Wars. They see themselves as the rebels and the US army as the empire. Everyone believes they're the hero. All their sins are for good reason, all their enemies are evil.

Something also needs to be said about the growing sense of entitlement and victim narrative that our country is believing. As I've worked with young kids, I have gotten to see it in it's beginning, and it's a difficult demon to exorcise. There are whole industries bent on convincing us that we're helpless and in need of rescue from our evil neighbors. Righteous victimhood feels gratifying for a time, but it makes you weak in the end. Even when people are genuinely against us, to place all the blame on them and none on ourselves will only make us powerless. As I say again and again to my students, find the part that's your fault, because that's the part you can fix. Dealing with a blamer is slow work, but we have to teach them to see the other person's perspective and then look for the part that's their fault.

To navigate conflict within families is much harder than the ones at school. There is a complicated history with the people you've lived with so long. That history is very difficult to keep out of conflicts that can seem so small from the outside. Blame and assuming are still ever present, but don't forget to set clear boundaries around criticism, defensiveness, stonewalling, and contempt. Left unattended, those four habits can destroy any relationship, and their presence can even be a highly correlated predictor of divorce when present in couples.

If you use any of these four habits to deal with (or really avoid) conflict, you are not only undermining your marriage, but you are handing your children a destructive set of habits for their own conflict, and planting dysfunction into their future. They are habits, rather than beliefs, and they all come from you giving yourself permission to mistreat the ones you love. If you teach your children the golden rule, you cannot use criticism, defensive counterattacks, stonewalling, and contempt or disgust when arguing with your spouse or your children. You can, but it makes you a liar because no one wants to be treated that way. There are many times and ways in which we are all liars, but nevertheless, there is a lot at stake here. It's time to sort this out and break these destructive habits.

IT'S NOT ALWAYS DEFIANCE

Besides having don'ts for arguing, what are some strategies you can use that will help you and your family walk away successfully having resolved disagreement? Remember that the goal of parenting teenagers is that they are able to make their own plans and complete them. So give honor to those plans, even if they're different than you would make. Give them the amount of respect you would give a friend or someone at work that you might oversee who tells you their plans. You may have to step in and change their direction, but always start from a place of value. That's the first rung of the ladder.

When you do get into conflict with your children, remember to separate their impulsive reactions from actual choices they make. If they are living in a power-struggling mind-set, then their behavior will be far more calculating (and frustrating) than kids who are impulsively saying and doing foolish things. And you need to deal with them differently. Don't forget that the first rule of dealing with impulse is to control your own impulses. Your stress becomes their stress, and when you start yelling, you're setting the rules of engagement that you can expect to see come back to you eventually.

If you face genuine defiance and a deliberate struggle for power, calm becomes even more important. To get someone out of that, you have to avoid falling into it yourself. As my mom used to say, it takes two to tango. Walking away and coming back when things have calmed down isn't the same as stonewalling. You're not saying that you don't want to talk about it, you're saying that you want that conversation to be respectful and productive. One communicates value and a standard of mutual respect. The other sets a dangerous precedent that painful things should be avoided.

People get stuck in a power-struggle mentality because they've avoided painful things in the first place. Bitterness (unresolved anger) is fuel for an unhealthy desire to control. That bitterness, like all anger, is armor, and it always comes from fear. Fear comes in three main forms: safety, rejection, and failure. Fear can sit unrecognized and unresolved for years, and when it does, it will spill poison into all your work and relationships. If you find anger coming up unexpectedly in your own life, it very likely means there are fears and pain you haven't worked through.

You can't go on thinking that your children's habits of anger and control are the real problem. Neither are yours. Anger and control are the armor you put on to protect you from fear, and fear is a poison to loving connection. Like all habits, anger and control can be changed with intense effort, but you need to recognize that they're coping mechanisms. If you take away their armor but not the fearful beliefs that inspire it, their souls will find other ways to protect themselves. The end of the road for power strugglers is a dark one.

As a young teacher, I remember a student named Jimmy who was convinced that every correction I gave him was a personal attack. He had a habit of talking a little bit longer than everyone else, so when the class had quieted down enough to teach, his voice would be the one ringing out. It got to the point that just saying his name brought him to instant rage, and his counterattack was to argue in front of the whole class. His anger and control were keeping him from feeling rejected by his teacher, and his goal was removal from the class. If you have to kick a kid out of class, there are many kids who see that as defeat on the teacher's part, giving up. They love to make the teacher give up, because they believe that's what you want to do anyway. I tried several strategies to help him believe that I wasn't out to get him, but I can't say I did that very well. I learned a lot in the process, and I still think about him often.

Sometimes your child brings the battle to you and won't relent. Very often, they do that at the moment when it's most socially difficult for you. That's partly because your own stress in those moments raises their anxiety immediately, but don't forget that embarrassing the person they're mad at is intensely satisfying. Attention seekers and power strugglers both love an audience, so the first step in dealing with them is to remove that audience. With my student, I learned that I had to send him in the hallway whenever he responded with an angry outburst. Once in the hall, it was actually very easy to deal with him if I gave him a bit of time to cool down. You can use the same strategy with your kids. "Go to your room" isn't a consequence (especially if their room is full of distractions and far from relational connection), but it can be a holding pattern for you to come to them and speak calmly and respectfully about your intent.

The practice of separation and calming down is training their brains to step away from conflict, rather than reacting and making it worse. Watch out for stonewalling, though. We don't allow it. We persist in conflict until restoration is achieved. Restoration is the goal of all discipline. Bad behavior is wrong because it separates us from each other. As parents, we are the interrupters and the restorers.

To train this process, which is very difficult for kids at the moment of anger and outburst, start by practicing obedience. The simplest first step is to teach kids to pause what they're doing and come to you. Practice it on them. When they're playing quietly nearby, call them over. Come here and get a hug. Come here and be encouraged. It's a simple step to establish the process of stopping what you're wanting to do to meet someone else's needs. It's simple submission to authority that builds relationship.

Then, try it when they're playing with friends or on a screen. They'll be more engaged, and it will be harder to tear themselves away from it. Also, start introducing simple tasks you want them to complete. Soon, you'll have a positive routine of obedience, so when there's a problem, they will naturally come to you and get corrected. Start a pattern of obedience and connection that includes correction. Because that's what loving parents do.

A good coach watches their team with the next game in mind. A great coach will coach for next year. What do they need to practice now so they can perform at the next level? What missing skills are causing frustration? Do they need encouragement or stern rebuke? Your kids need you to be that coach for them. If you fall into the same routine of failure and discipline, it will end up with resentment in you and them. If you establish a picture of what it will be like for them at the next level, you can start preparing them for it now.

There are a hundred more ways to support kids in their struggle. There are lists from websites all over. The big idea is that strategic support is an expression of the genuine affection you laid down as a foundation. You've convinced them that your discipline is for them and not you, that you care about how well they are doing. Now you need to prove it. Look for the places they're falling down and teach them to watch their step in those places. If the steps to success are too high for them to master, then break each process into smaller pieces.

CHAPTER 10

HIGH EXPECTATIONS

HABITS
HIGH EXPECTATIONS
STRATEGIC SUPPORT
GENUINE AFFECTION
BELIEFS

We are building a ladder that our children can climb to bring them into a problem-solving mentality. The final rung of the ladder is high expectations that produces real performance. You've established your genuine affection, and you know it will be tested, but that doesn't stop you. You've looked at where they repeatedly fall down, and you've found the stumbling blocks that need to be moved or warned about. You've kept them from failing too much, but you haven't removed the challenges or kept them as babies. Now it's time to be the coach.

In the previous chapter we talked about triangulating your expectations and consequences with your children so you're not seen as a referee in their life. There are plenty of referees out there calling fouls and telling people when they've failed. What they don't have is a lot of quality coaches who believe in them and want them to improve. Not the throwing chairs type of coach, either. Kids and adults alike need coaches who see their strengths and their weaknesses and still put them in the game.

EAGER TO PLEASE

I once heard a story about a teenager whose dad came to see her perform in the school play. After the show, the girl came out into the theater's foyer to greet her family. Her mom gave her an excited hug and they talked about how the great show went. Her dad looked on in quiet confidence. After a minute or two, her mom walked away to say hi to a friend and the teenager looked at her dad, waiting for him to praise her performance. Finally she asked the most important man in her life what he thought of the performance. "It was all right." he said, "there are a few things you could have improved." Without a hint of disgust or amazement he told her simply what he thought.

"Why can't you just say it was great?" She replied with frustration. "That's what mom always says."

He looked her in the eyes and asked, "Whose opinion matters more to you?" and gave her a pat on the back and looked around the crowded foyer. She knew he was right. He was simply giving her honest feedback, and that made his input so much more valuable.

———

Life itself is really what raises the bar. It's not your authority, or that of others, that make your children feel inadequate. They are ashamed, in part, because they don't know if they have what it takes to meet the demands of a harsh world. Will they choke in the most important moment? Will they crumble beneath the pressure? You can try to keep training wheels on them, but then they'll never know if they can be tough. They will only pretend they are. There are a lot of pretenders out there, hoping no one sees their true self, but your kids don't have to be among them. High expectations are vital.

Many people offer compassion without high expectations. They talk often of empathy, but what they mean is low expectations, and they try to combat shame with empty compliments. If shame says that you're not good enough, empathetic low-expecters want to counter that with high praise. What they don't understand is that compliments almost never sink below the conscious mind, where shame lives. Shame is a deeply held belief that was formed without your conscious understanding.

Effective high-expecters know that the opposite of shame isn't arrogance, but confidence, and it comes from overcoming real adversity repeatedly. That's the only way to build it. When kids learn to succeed in difficult circumstances, then they learn that they have what it takes, at least for now. Those difficult circumstances may even be created by you, and that's even better. Then you'll be there to help them learn from whatever failures they encounter.

I say "effective" high-expecters because there are plenty who are totally ineffective and even destructive. High expectation is a difficult game to play well, and a family is much different than a sports team or business venture. In the latter cases, coaches and players have something that they all want: to win. Any of those players or employees can leave whenever they want, and they can also be cut from the team. Teachers and parents don't have that luxury, if you can even call it that.

There is no easy score to keep for childhood, no enemy. The goal is contentment and growth, trust and generosity. The enemy is the chaos within each of us, and the excuses we make for allowing it to grow. No one is keeping score, because how could you? It's a journey more than a war, and when raising your children feels like combat, it usually means you're doing it wrong.

The old Bible verse gets it right when it says, "Our battle is not against flesh and blood." The battle really is against the beliefs and habits that are sabotaging your children's potential, and it comes down to whether you have the strength to stand in one place with your feet on the truth. Will you refuse to give in to the drama and manipulation that fear and blame are spewing on you? You can't defeat them any other way. When it feels like you've done everything you can to help your kids, you've told them the truth again and again with all the patience you can muster, then just stand firm.

With each new phase of childhood and adolescence, your children's awareness of the world grows. With that growth comes a new insecurity to be faced, a bigger fear. Often that insecurity will show itself just when you think they've grown out of it: impulsive, needy, and fearful behavior starts all over again. To resolve it, they need discipline. Not in the punishing sense, but in the determined effort brings growth sense.

Discipline in the face of insecurity is the seed of confidence. Plant those seeds by supporting them to meet the higher bar life brings.

Living up to high expectations and creating a place of repeated victory will quiet the fear of failure to a manageable tone. No matter how much victory you attain, it won't silence fear, but it's a beginning. Building emotional strength in the face of fear is not about making the fear disappear. It's more about building the courage to face that fear until it seems small in comparison to your own willpower.

EXPOSURE THERAPY

When psychologists work with people suffering from a variety of anxieties or phobias, one commonly accepted method is exposure therapy. This form of behavior therapy involves exposing people to incrementally more significant doses of the object of their fear. If, for example, your fear was public speaking, which combines rejection and failure in one, then you would first be asked to imagine speaking in front of a small crowd. Keep imagining until it's boring. Perhaps then you might be asked to speak in front of one person. If that went well, you would then speak in front of 4 people. On and on you'd go until you reached a sizeable crowd, having become adjusted to the fear.

The fear may not go away at all, but your confidence is now stronger. The psychologist's goal is to create a series of victories in the face of your fear. Exposure therapy has been found to be effective for a wide variety of fears and mental health conditions ranging from PTSD to general anxiety disorder. But it's not just for counselors. Effective coaches use it too.

Coaches can't change the rules of the game. In fact, they don't want to. If you made baskets easier to score, not only would you not be playing basketball anymore, you wouldn't be rising to the challenge. More importantly, you'd be falling short of your own potential. A coach wants to equip you for the game by setting you up to push yourself beyond what you think you can handle. You don't want to push so far that you hurt yourself or quit (even if you might want to). Lifting heavy things makes you stronger, and your children's willpower works the same way. High expectations communicate your belief in their potential.

So why don't you hold your kids to high expectations? Perhaps the real reason is that you don't believe in them. You still think of them as the little kid who skinned their knee and came crying to you for comfort. You don't think they can do it, so you shield them from the inevitable failure they will face. If that's the case, then you best just say it and lower the bar. Failure is a real issue you have to overcome as a high-expecter. Kids who lack skills are going to fail, and they better get used to it. That's why they need you. The first lesson of high expectations is to lean into the pain of failure.

To build up their strength, you have to keep the right balance between success and quitting. Quitting is a trap, and once you step into it you will find it pulling you back again and again. On the other side of that balance is too much success, and the mediocrity and stagnation that come with it. There's a life of regret over there if you're not careful. You need failure because without it there's no learning. If you had all the answers and could do all the stuff, then why would you go to school? How would you learn and grow? But too much failure is a poison.

As a high school kid, I learned this lesson the hard way. As an underclass man, I was a terrible wrestler, but I remember deciding that I would not be a quitter. So I wrestled for three years. I was so full of fear of failure that my nerves on the day of a match would make me sick. By the time I stepped on the mat, I was already exhausted and dreading the six minutes that lay ahead. I remember times when I was relieved to be pinned early in the match just to get it over with. My freshman year I didn't win a single match. I didn't get much better as time went on, and I really grew to hate the sport over the three years I competed. Only after suffering from a recurring back injury did I feel like I was free to switch sports. So I joined my friends and become a swimmer.

Swimming was something I did for fun and not obligation. I loved the challenge and the work, but I with absolutely no pressure on myself to excel. No one was telling me (including myself) that if I failed it meant I wasn't valuable. I had nothing to prove so it was much easier to push myself to a high standard. As a wrestler, I was the only one telling me to prove I was a good enough, but I was just stuck in a proving mind-set in that setting and it kept me from enjoying it or doing well.

When I became a swimmer, I discovered that I actually could be quite a good athlete. In fact, a friend who had been on the team for years told me that because I was a first year swimmer I couldn't get good. It was all the fuel I needed. Without a fear of failure, I pushed myself harder than I ever knew I could. I started in the slowest lane on the team and week after week worked my way up to faster groups. The pool was split in half, with a coach on each side, and within a month I was in the fastest lane on the slow side. I remember looking over to the other side and thinking that I had done pretty well and could take it easy for the rest of the season. I am certain that had I been protecting or covering a frail ego that's what I might have done.

Instead, I went to that fast side of the pool and suffered. For the first couple weeks I was gripping the edge of the pool between sets trying not to throw up. By the end of the season I was able to swim among the fastest group. I did the backstroke in the varsity relay and made it on the all-time team leaderboard for my events. It was no state championship, but it was one of the biggest lessons in my life. If you love something, you will excel at it far more than if you do it because you don't want to be a failure. It was my first big experience enjoying sports after many years of failure and insecurity.

As a first year teacher, years removed from that wrestling room, my principal told me that the wrestling team needed coaches or there wouldn't be a team. Reluctantly I agreed to help out. As a 23 year old, I was a year younger than the head coach, and only 5 years older than the senior wrestlers. When I stepped on the mat as a coach, something strange happened. I found that I kind of liked the sport, and I wasn't that bad at it. When there was nothing to prove, nothing on the line, I could compete with the best kids on our team. Not only that, but I loved coaching like I loved teaching. I was pushing kids to learn and strive and maybe find their potential.

Later that year, I remember hearing a coach say that the reason we were there was that every kid has a fail meter that tells them when they have reached their limit. The coach's job is to show them that their meter is wrong. You can do more than you think.

I have a vivid memory of our preparations for the district meet, with kids working as hard as they had all year in hopes of getting to the state tournament. I was watching a young kid wrestling an older, heavier wrestler again and again. He was exhausted, a bit of blood dripping out of his nose from getting slammed by someone's arm, and crying. But he was not stopping. He didn't quit because he had a coach who genuinely loved him, was helping him in his weaknesses, and who knew there was more in there than he realized. He made it to state.

The truth is, we all need coaches. We all need our fail meter adjusted because we don't know what we're capable of, and we'll never find out without someone holding us to a high standard. He was getting worked over in hopes that when he faced kids his own weight, they would seem light.

THE WORLD NEEDS CRITICS

As a teacher, I would put kids into groups. That works great when they are excited to discuss a big idea or teach each other concepts at a higher level. It stinks when half the group wants to do nothing and one or two kids end up doing all the work. In order to get around that, I created recurring jobs. One kid was the time keeper, another read the instructions, etc. The best job, I thought, was the critic. Their job was to make sure the group wasn't going in the wrong direction. If I approached a group who misunderstood the directions or had gotten off track, I turned to the critic to figure out why they weren't doing their job.

Critical thinking is a vital skill, and one that most classroom teachers are not equipped to develop in your child. It's your job to teach them to think, and there is no better place than the dinner table. We each need to be properly critical of ourselves, the ideas we encounter, and the habits we've formed, otherwise we won't grow. If our children can honestly evaluate their own strengths and weaknesses, and handle it when others do the same, then they will be miles ahead of their peers. They almost certainly will be thought of as leaders wherever they go.

If you're not careful, however, your kids will become their own worst critic. Shame is the collection of internalized referees, so it's very important to minimize how often your voice gets added to the mix. No matter how hard you try, there will be things you say which will haunt your children, but try you must. Many of the negative beliefs we carry about ourselves come from our parents. As we've discussed at length in this book, shame will keep coming back for the rest of their lives. Don't be shame fuel, but also remember that we need to equip them to handle failure, not avoid it.

One of the worst things I hear parents, teachers, and media say to kids is that they are perfect the way they are. That's not only untrue, but it stunts their growth and ends up creating hopelessness and a victim mentality. If they don't need to grow or change, and they're only ten years old (or 25), then two terrible conclusions follow: First, all the world's problems become someone else's fault (society, culture, the system). Because I'm as good as I could ever hope to be, then the world's suffering can't be my fault. Second, what hope do I have of making an impact in the world? I can't fix the world now, and I'll never get any better, so my only hope is to gain positions of power to force people to do the right thing. The system is at fault, so I must become the ruler of the system. Power and influence become the highest ideal.

Everybody wants the world to improve, but we forget that it only does so when we each improve individually. Self-improvement is the real secret to healthy relationships, and society is just the collection of all our relationships. The victim mentality, however, is a poison. It tells you that nothing you do matters. That's fun when you want to misbehave, because hey, it doesn't matter. It's horrible when you want to fix anything, because, once more, nothing matters. The victim mentality, when it runs its course, ends in a desire to destroy everything. We want our kids to take the road to empowerment, which starts with an honest assessment of success and failure.

SHARE YOUR PURPOSE

Your kids need to see that you're following your own purpose, pushing back against your own fears, and growing where you need to. Wanting to improve so you won't feel bad about your laziness, or obesity, or smoking, isn't enough. That's trying to use shame as a motivator, and as a rule it stinks at that job. What you need is a purpose bigger than yourself, and your kids need one too.

Sharing that purpose also shows them that you're not perfect, and that your boundaries and authority aren't based on moral superiority. I can't tell you how many times I've heard people trying to hide their youthful foolishness because they thought it would take away their credibility with their teenagers. The opposite effect is true. You must show them your failures, and that you're facing them, if you expect them to do the same. You've learned from the past, sometimes the hard way, so that they don't have to. Share your regrets so your kids can avoid them. Hide your regrets and your kids will fall for the same trap you did when you were their age.

You can't stop at self-improvement. Your community needs you. Your family needs you. Remember that every relationship you improve makes the world a better place. Everyone you forgive, every bitter memory you let go of, makes a little more peace in your home, and therefore in your neighborhood. You also can't wait until your problems are solved before you help others. You're only a hypocrite if you think the rules don't apply to you. An imperfect person who aims for the highest ideal is the best you can hope for. Don't denigrate it. There are no perfect people, but we should all aim for perfection.

In many ways your purpose and your children's will overlap. When you set out to improve your neighborhood, it might include their school. You can ask your children how they are going to improve their school, or are they just a participant? This will result in both you and them taking on leadership roles, but only indirectly. The goal is to help, and the best leaders are the most helpful to the most people. The worst leaders are motivated by ego as a way to cover up their fearful shame. They see people as objects to be controlled. It's important to make that distinction, because true purpose is selfless. You are taking on a task that's bigger than yourself, and done correctly, it will bring you deeper into a community of like-minded people.

Creativity is unleashed when you truly dive into such purpose. Not necessarily painting a masterpiece or writing a sonnet, but the type of creativity that thinks of problems as opportunities. Solving a puzzle or brain teaser is creative too. A math word problem requires creativity. They all require seeing the world in a new way and being open to solutions that you haven't considered before. When you find a purpose larger than yourself, it unleashes something inside you. That's part of thinking like a problem solver, and it's what the world needs more of.

If a missionary is just a person with a mission, then what would it take to put your whole family on mission? One process that I've seen help is to write out the mission your family is on. How could you activate your children's imagination and effort to improve themselves as they aim for something higher? What's special about missionaries is that they aren't tied down by the same patterns that everyone else feels stuck to. They are foreigners who bring some better idea to share. What if your family could feel that way without leaving home? What good idea could you share if you weren't tied down by the expectations of your friend group? Start by writing down the idea and put it on the wall or refrigerator. Change it, adjust it, use it. After two weeks, if you haven't talked about it, it has effectively disappeared from view. It's going take work, but it's worth it.

Being on mission means bearing the weight of more than just yourself. How can you bear the weight of the wrongs and dysfunction of the people on your street or in your neighborhood? What about your town or county? It's nice to talk to kids about changing the world, but the only thing that makes the world better is people caring for each other deliberately. That has to happen one person at a time. Don't get overly complicated. It comes down to serving more, gossiping less, and doing the good things that need to be done. Social and political activism simply aren't making the change that are needed in our world. Government programs cannot replace the work of people who care. I say that having worked for the government for 15 years.

Effective change requires loving people willing to reach out beyond their self-interest. I don't mean loving in the sense the they are full of warm feelings about the strangers next door. Perhaps they are, but they're willing to sacrifice their own comfort to invest in something that lasts longer than the tv series they've been enjoying, or the vacation they saved up for. Invest in your family, then your neighborhood.

In the small community where we live, there is a Mennonite church on the traditional end of the spectrum. More Amish than Evangelical, but they still drive nice trucks. The women wear dresses they make themselves, the men work with their hands in a variety of blue collar occupations, and they rely on each other in a remarkable way. My family has had the opportunity to know a few of them and visit their church, and we're always struck by their peaceful and honest way of life.

The Mennonite families send their kids to a private school that their church runs, and after eighth grade the kids all go to work with their parents. They learn a trade and support their families. For the vast majority of human history, this type of system was the norm. I don't know if America could manage that sort of thing on a large scale, but you can help your children become part of your family's purpose. Give them a mission of their own, with lots of support. Teach them to resist the urge to fail/quit that will inevitably come, and it will motivate them far more than allowances or threats of punishment.

While the Mennonites in my community have marked out an old-fashioned way of life, the world marches on. There is no telling what the working world will be like in 20 years. Technology, cultural change, and global politics seem more chaotic than ever. Industries are changing at a rapid pace. What brings value to a company today may be completely different in 20 years, and you will need to adapt. That adaptation is based on finding what's broken and fixing it. Your kids will only be able to do that long term if they've found their own creative purpose and are working toward it in their career.

Knowing that, a creative mentality is what your kids need, and they likely won't be learning it in school. Part of your job as a parent will be to give them those skills. But the standard model of chores is just the beginning. Chores help you instill concern for the household, you hope, but it can also become drudgery. Bring kids into the vision you have for yourself, and invite them to find one of their own. Entrepreneurship is a simple way to organize that. When they make money, they very clearly can measure their success.

Don't think that your purpose is just setting goals for yourself and your kids, though that's not a bad start. At the very least, set habits that can last a lifetime. Figure out what it takes to grow into the person you want to be, and ask them to do the same thing. What kind of leader do they want to be in their work life, community, and family? That kind of thinking requires a long-term investment into becoming a person of character and emotional strength. It's emotionally strong people who can save the world by bearing the weight of other people's dysfunction and establishing order where there in only chaos.

When it comes to family, remember as well that it's not about finding Mr. or Ms. Right. Help your sons and daughters throw out the modern fairy tale of finding "the one" who really understands them. What they actually need is a formidable spouse. Someone they can wage war with. A teammate who resolves conflict without quitting. If they find such a man or woman, will they be ready to team up? A huge part of the purpose of adolescence is becoming someone worth marrying. You may not describe it that way, but remember that it's very likely that the vast majority of their life will be in a marriage relationships, so the work you do as a parent in the 20-30 years before marriage is just the first chapters of a long story. Will their story be mostly joy or mostly heartache?

Your habits and beliefs together form the character that will make for successful relationships the rest of your life, in every area. Your ability to hold yourself to a high standard, and above all things to not quit, that's what it takes to be a good spouse, someone worth marrying. That person isn't going to want anything to do with your kids if they can't be relied upon.

Chapter 11

GROW UP WITH THEM

I f failure is part of the process, then part of your job as a coach is to show them how it's done. As your kids enter middle school and their teenage years, it's time to start being honest about your own efforts to grow, and to stop hiding your own need for improvement. As I mentioned in the last chapter, many parents have denied their own weaknesses for fear of rejection or criticism and built kids who think authority figures are hypocrites. When your kids are little, they think you know so much and have so much experience. As they get older, they will begin to see the cracks in that image. Don't hide it. Don't get defensive. Bring them into your process of growth.

What you're doing is establishing for them a pattern of growth and learning that will last a lifetime. Perhaps you're reading this thinking that you have so many faults, and so little strength to fix them. How can you share that with your children? I'm here to tell you that you don't have to. They are already seeing it. If they are over the age of ten, they are seeing more of your dysfunction every day. The question is whether they will have grace or judgment to offer you in return. As they get older and begin to see friends' families seem so perfect, the comparison and resentment will begin. I know it's true because I remember doing it. I was that resentful kid.

For several years of my adolescence, my family was always on the verge of chaos. My parents' marriage was falling apart, and my brothers and I each struggled in our own way. We longed to find our place in our home, church, and school. At the end of those painful years, I watched as my mom and dad worked through their pain together. With the help of people willing to step in and help them clean up their mess, they not only forgave each other, but they were transformed into a couple who was dedicated to helping bear the weight for other people's broken marriages.

In the midst of all the chaotic years, I distinctly remember going to a friends' house. His parents made more money than mine, they had a nice house on the hill, and everything about his life seemed perfect. His room was cleaner than mine, his family's minivan didn't have food wrappers or old socks in it (none of them were mine, I swear). His garage could fit a car in it, for crying out loud, and he had a hot tub. I was never more resentful of my family than when I came home from his house to my own. It didn't matter to me that my family was living out a story of redemption, nor could I see my part in helping that story along. All I could see is that he had what I wanted, and it wasn't fair.

It doesn't matter how polished or messy your life is at this moment. What your kids need is for the parents they have to show them how everyone makes mistakes, and everyone grows if they try. The message of high expectations is that you're not okay how you are, but if we love and support each other, then it will get better. Don't just take your place of authority and push them to step up. Invite them into the process of crafting the growth of your whole family. Ask for their input on more than where you go camping or what's for dinner. Talk about the purpose of community and service, and then do something about it. Talk about your own personal improvement efforts and struggles. Set your course together, so they'll know how to do the same for their family one day, and then their communities and businesses.

Credibility with teenagers is built through honest interactions where their perspectives are shown the same respect as your own. If your child is in the midst of a power struggling mentality, especially when it comes to you, then it's going to be a rocky beginning. Asking them for input will be met with skepticism at best, and more likely sarcasm and contempt. Don't get drawn into a battle. Ask the honest questions and wait for honest answers. It may not happen the first time, or the fifth, but trust takes time to develop.

If you've been using your authority to demand control, what you're getting is fear. That's different, and it isn't a relationship. Perhaps you've worked at a job where someone used their position that way. It's not good, and the first things to disappear when one demands control is trust and creativity. Trust and creativity are the goal of every working relationship, and that's what you're trying to develop with your teenager.

That doesn't mean that you put up with mockery or defiance. It means you deal with it in a way that still communicates that they are a valuable person. Remember that your ladder stands on the solid ground of staying calm, and they will never believe you love them if you treat them like they're worthless.

What mockery and defiance are showing is genuine emotion and unresolved conflict. It may not even be with you. Those emotions, and whatever that conflict is, it matters as long as they matter. Their terrible way of communicating is the real problem, and it's a bad habit that can only be changed with calm feedback. Just like teaching them to stop eating their boogers when they were little. Screaming at them might stop the behavior for a while, but it also puts a big wall between you and tears down your credibility in the long run.

You have to earn trust, just like they do. If your children have been telling themselves a story of victimhood and ill-intent, then it will be even slower to begin to correct their course. If you've been engaging in the power struggle with them, with your own outbursts of anger and flexing of muscle, then you have been feeding that narrative. High standards are not just limited to your children's behavior. They should also apply to you. Are you holding yourself to a high standard of parenting? Are you improving? They can tell.

It's funny how much we separate our relationships with our kids from the ones we have everywhere else. I have had more than one conversation with teachers and staff asking them what the circumstances are where they need me, as their boss, to yell at them. Invariably, their answer is that there is none, and we agree that we shouldn't be yelling at our students either. The way you want to be treated by people in authority over you is a good marker for how you should treat your kids, even when they're teenagers.

There are limits to that metaphor, of course, but not many. Once your kids are about 8 years old, perhaps, then their opinions and reflections should hold about the same weight as you would give to any adult you might be in authority over. That doesn't mean they are in charge, because they are kids after all, but their perspective has to matter to you. If you disagree, you should do so respectfully. If you hurt their feelings, you should say you're sorry.

Saying sorry is one of the best trust builders you have, if you really mean it. Everyone knows that the test of a genuine apology is how much the behavior repeats, and kids have a great ability to smell a fake. Apologizing about your bad habits (like yelling) only goes so far if you're not getting better at fixing it. Tell them that, that you're working to change it, but it's a bad habit and you're going to fail at times. Kids won't be very good at seeing a pattern of improvement either, so they may need your help to see it.

DON'T CALL THEM SMART

One common technique parents and teachers both use when they want to defeat shame is to praise them for being smart, or pretty, or talented. This often comes in the form of praising them for simple things anyone else their age can do. Acting like it proves they're special and skilled is never convincing. They have been comparing themselves to others from an early age, so they know exactly how talented or pretty they are. The only thing that telling them they're special will convince them of is that either you don't know what you're talking about, or you're a liar. In both situations, that means they can't rely on you in the future.

I have a good friend who was excited to raise his daughter well. Unfortunately, he got some bad advice on this subject. Someone told him that daughters need to hear they're beautiful from their dad so they won't go looking for it from a boy. So that's what he did, in public and private, on social media and in person, he and his wife repeatedly told her she was beautiful. Like the kids who are told they're smart for the simplest tasks, their daughter knew exactly how pretty she was, and saw all her imperfections. With every compliment, her inner critic pointed out every flaw. She began to see her dad as either ignorant or dishonest, his opinion unreliable. It put the question of physical appearance repeatedly at the center of her thinking, and thus her priorities.

What that advice was trying to fulfill was the need all children have to know they matter to their dad. What it was missing was the idea that beauty comes from within, value comes from character, not from looks, talent, or intelligence. No father should be modeling his praise on what selfish teenage boys care about. Every child, son or daughter, has a need for value. The question becomes where they will look for it. In the case of my friend, when he doubled down on the question of beauty, his daughter grew up believing and fearing the answer. She fell for the traps that are common among her peers: endless selfies online with flaw-fixing photo apps, chasing boys who, like her father, talked about looks over substance. If her dad couldn't love her for what was inside, maybe those boys would.

Some people think that is the reason celebrities are so fragile and prone to self-destruction. They're surrounded by people who sing their praises for talent, beauty, and popularity. All things they can't control. If that's the thing everyone notices, then it must be the most important thing in the world. If the things that get you love and belonging (or the cheap substitute: fame) is something you can't change, then you're completely powerless. Every setback, no matter how small, chips away at your all-important image. You only care about what people say you are, even when you know its not the truth.

There's evidence that calling kids smart, or otherwise praising them for qualities that seem to be outside their control, reinforces their own fear of failure and makes them more likely to quit when they face difficulty. One landmark study of this phenomenon was conducted on fifth graders taking a math test. A group of students were each given a test that was two years below where they were currently performing. Randomly, kids were told by the proctor that they had done well and they "must be really smart," or "they must have worked really hard." That statement, said once by a stranger in a lab coat, had a huge effect.

Kids were each then given a math test that was two years above where they performed. On this test they naturally performed poorly. Each child was then given the option to return to the easier work or persist in learning how to do the more challenging work they had just failed on. The kids who were told they were smart were far more likely to want to retreat from the challenging work and retake the easier test. Being praised for effort, however, set a different tone for the whole enterprise. One statement was all it took to establish that in this environment we are recognized for hard work. We don't give up because even if we fail, we can learn from our mistakes. Learning and growing is the point.

How well are you setting the tone in your household? Do kids get praised for being talented or gifted? Chances are good that that kind of praise is contributing to burn out later on. I've seen athletes on track for the Olympics quit because they couldn't take all the talk of their potential. I've seen middle schoolers doing college-level calculus start crying when they didn't get a concept quick enough. I've seen girls hate what they see in the mirror and tear each other down for not being perfect. They were all facing the same question of whether they have what it takes. If smarts, talent, or beauty is what you praise, then that is what you care about. Anything that threatens that, threatens your relationship with them. You can say that it doesn't, but your praise speaks volumes.

Early in my years as a principal, I had little more than my own teaching experience to guide me on the journey toward instructional improvement. I took over leadership of an elementary school that was struggling with a staff who were unkind to each other, and students who couldn't perform academically. I had taught middle and high school math and science, and here I was coaching and supporting teachers who needed to know how to teach the step by steps of reading. I was in over my head.

That first year, we had a phenomenal trainer come to our district, Dr. Anita Archer. She is a retired teacher who had dedicated her time to learning about and helping schools, especially classroom teachers, improve. She spoke about engaging strategies that turned the traditional lecture style into something that kids couldn't opt out of. For me, her most memorable story was about learning to play the cello.

As a retiree, she decided that she needed to keep learning. One thing she'd always wanted to pursue was playing the cello. She took a lesson each week at an instructor's studio, and the person whose lesson always came before her was a 9-year-old girl who was playing at a professional level. Each week, Dr. Archer would sit in the hall listening to this girl rehearse, and then she would hear the parents come to pick her up. The tutor and the parents alike would praise the little girl endlessly for her gifting and talent, while the veteran teacher just shook her head.

Sure enough, after many weeks of this, the little girl announced that she was quitting. She would no longer practice or take lessons. The tutor and the parents were devastated, and Dr. Archer could no longer stay silent. In her feisty, lovable way, she stepped into the studio from the hall and asked if she could offer her advice. Stop praising her for her talent. Praise her for her hard work. That's what got her here, and that's the only thing she can control. She can't change how talented she it, and if that's all you praise, then that's what she thinks you care about. Give her space, praise her hard work, and see if she doesn't come back and want to play.

Sure enough, within a few weeks, the little girl was back. Dr. Archer sat in the hall and listened as the parents and the tutor recognized her hard work. They all watched as the little girl blossomed before their eyes, ready to pursue a creative purpose free from the proving mentality that poisons our best efforts.

IF THEY CAN, THEY SHOULD

Sometimes, as parents, some part of us wants our children to stay weak. Perhaps we miss the feeling of being intensely needed by an innocent child, or maybe we aren't willing to face the conflict that high expectations so often require. So we don't mind bringing them the water bottle they keep forgetting, or tying their shoes for them as they busily look at our phone (I've seen it with teenagers). When we protect our kids from the disappointment and sadness of failure, we are keeping them weak. In the end, they'll resent us for it, and in the meantime they'll be unprepared for the pain and failure that life will bring.

We all have inside us a needy, attention-seeking parent we have to silence. We miss those days of nurturing, and we hate the stress of holding high expectations. We respond impulsively to our children's immature behavior, sometimes avoiding, sometimes exploding. We hope our kids will fulfill our need to believe we're a "good mom" or a "father who knows best." But it's not their job to make you feel okay, and your impulsive reactions are making it harder for them to grow. The bottom line is that needy parenting is emotional weakness, and you're raising your kids to see parenting the same way. If you're going to adjust their fail meter, then you'll need to adjust your own. It will definitely require strength. Stand firm on the truth. They need you.

A big part of that confidence-building process is to say yes when they form their own plans. Making a plan and completing it is a complex set of thinking skills. It requires prediction of future events (pretty easy), with accountability for accuracy (much harder). A good plan will predict how difficult something will be, it will consider the perspective of others, what might go wrong, and how both things will be handled. All these questions can be asked by a parent with high expectations who is looking for ways to give value to their child. We want to build kids who can think.

After you've gone through some version of the planning process, let them do the plan. If you're the coach in their lives whose opinion they look up to, then your approval of their plans will be priceless. Don't stop them all the time. The plan might be a waste of time, or it may be the harder way of doing something, but if it's not dangerous or expensive, try to say yes. They will feel valuable, to be sure, but they will also learn from it, and that's the goal of high expectations. Follow up with them and ask how it went. Was it as hard or easy as you thought? How would you change your plan if you did it again? How well did it go, and why do you think so? It doesn't take long, and you're on to the next thing.

This process will bring you back to the strategic support as well. If all their plans are failures, or they're too complex to complete (another version of failure), then they will soon stop making them. That's not the lesson we're trying to teach. Remember, confidence comes from a track record of success in the face of real challenges. To get that confidence, your strategic support is to make sure the plan is doable, and you need to be prepared to step in for guidance. If anything, this is the hardest part when their plans are more like nonsense. Going on a long bike ride is one thing, starting a small business is quite another. I've made the mistake of over estimating how much of my own time and effort were needed to pull off a plan, and then looked on in frustration when the plan didn't work out. I have to wonder if that means that the plan in question was more my plan than theirs.

I often find myself wishing that my kids were the self-starting entrepreneurs, or more determined and passionate about some challenging but rewarding skill. That may come, but it's important to remember that you aren't trying to change their personality, which is what much of that is about. You're trying to develop character and peacefulness. Can they solve problems? Do they persist in difficult tasks or when resolving disagreements? Are they peacemakers in a hostile world? Are they helpful? These are the things that every community needs and every person can provide.

CHAPTER 12

AIM SMALL, HIT SMALL

My brother-in-law is an avid hunter and marksman. He's intensely competitive about everything he does, but in a fun way. Where others want to dominate or avoid the competition out of fear of failure, Jon makes it into a game and invites everyone to play. The difference with him is that when everyone else has tried the game and realized how well they can do, he keeps going. His goal is to reach his highest possible level of performance. Again and again he'll aim or race or whatever we're doing, and he'll pursue his best.

He has taken that ability to focus into a wide variety of pursuits, and in each area he doesn't just beat his friends and celebrate. In fact, he hardly celebrates. He works and works until he fulfills his actual potential. It's incredible to watch because he's not obsessing over failure or avoiding losses. He is having fun and pursuing his potential. I want to be more like Jon.

One of Jon's pursuits is marksmanship. He's an avid hunter and competitive shooter. In the few times we've shot targets together, Jon's advice is always the same: aim small, hit small. If you're satisfied with a big target, then that's all you'll ever hit. If you're satisfied with a smaller target, your aim will improve. If you aim for the exact location of your previous shot again and again, from ever increasing distances, and you keep going when everyone else quits, then you just might be the best.

That's how I want to parent my kids. Not that I want to drive them to be their best, though a little of that is really good. I want to drive myself to be the best parent I can be. I want to work through my thoughts and beliefs and get them all in line with my values. I want my habits to be strong and set me right, and not fall into the failures of my past. I'm not satisfied with being a better parent than anyone else, in fact that's not my aim. My goal is the be the absolute best parent I can be, to reach my potential.

When you set out to make a shift in how you think of yourself as a parent, not to mention how your kids think about themselves and the world around them, you need to set your priorities. There are a lot of things I've talked about in this book that you simply won't be able to accomplish right away. What are the most important, and most impactful first steps you can make as a parent? You need a target for your aim.

In most targets, there is a bullseye and concentric rings surrounding it. Each ring is incrementally larger, but the total area of the biggest circle is exponentially larger than that of the ones within. If you aim for the center, you may still hit the target, even if you miss your mark. As a beginner, that's okay and expected. Your goal is to improve over time, even as you aim for the same bullseye.

FIRST MAKE A DIFFERENCE

As a dad, I got roped into being the soccer coach for my son's team a few years ago. I don't know a lot about soccer, but I figured YouTube would help me. One thing I do know about sports, and what I told my players, was not to listen when people tell you it doesn't matter whether you win or lose. Of course it matters. It also matters how you play the game. Play fair, play to win.

This idea that we shouldn't keep score is common among parents of young kids, but it is remarkable how quickly it disappears when they get older. We don't mind them being losers when they're little (but they do), and then suddenly, when they're older, that seems to be all we care about. I don't know how long it's been since you sat in the stands of a high school sport, but the parents are often more obsessed and out-spoken than the kids.

We need to get our messaging straight. The same philosophy of winning and losing should be taught and abided by throughout their lives. Winning matters, and building each other up matters. Let's not get them on a pendulum at an early age, where they see sports as the source of their self-loathing and the opportunity for domination. Do your best to win, deal with your losses. Be a good sport in both circumstances. That's what kids need, and it's what parents need too.

We need to be able to admit when we're losing as parents, or failing rather. When we aren't effective, let's face it together and set out to make improvements. That would take a lot of honesty and trust between you and your spouse in order to get there. Your marriage may need to grow quite a bit first. Face that too. The first, largest ring of the circle that you need to hit in order to even get into the target is effectiveness. If you're not making a difference, then what's the use? As parents, we have to be honest with ourselves about that fact. Our purpose isn't here just to make us feel good about ourselves and get rid of insecurity.

There are many measures of success you can start with as a parent. It's tempting to start with the bad habits that your children exhibit. That's not a bad strategy, but don't get bogged down. Behind every bad habit is a destructive belief that will be much more difficult to root out. Your first area of effectiveness should probably be about yourself anyway. That's the thing you can change. Ask yourself how well you're avoiding the power struggle. How often are you taking their misbehavior personally? How often are you raising your voice or jumping to conclusions? How much do you interrupt them when correcting them? These are all bad habits you can begin to change right now.

There are several techniques you can use for improving and avoiding such things. Little methods of triangulation to take yourself out of the referee mode that we often fall into. Saying, "Yes, when…" instead of "No" is an easy start. "Yes, you can have another turn on the computer when your chores are done." Or "Yes, you can go outside to play when you've changed out of your pajamas." Step around the conflict when it's not necessary to fight.

"Try again," is another easy habit to pick up. Say it when kids are overreacting to each other or you. "Try again with a calm voice." Interrupting their attitudes without a lecture or guilt trip is wonderful. This is especially effective with their words. When they are too emotional and negative in their voice, the act of calming your voice down is actually calming in itself. Try it yourself sometime. Announce that you're going to try again too. It can completely change the tone of your household.

Another habit is thankfulness and recognition. The most effective leaders you've had in your life were very likely good at giving meaningful thanks at the right time. They didn't overdo it, but they noticed your efforts and it made your work so much easier. Do the same for your kids. Make a mental note of how often you're thanking them for the things they do. If you want them to put their dishes away without being asked, thank them for doing it when you do ask. Then watch like a hawk and make a big deal out of their work. Be their biggest cheerleader for those ten seconds and you'll gain hours of effort and trust.

Above all, the first big circle of this target of effective parenting is to compete against yourself. Take an honest look at your abilities as a parent and set out to change the habits that need to be changed, the things that are making your kids weak. Goals are nice, but these changes shouldn't be based on measurable, time-based shifts in behavior. You're going for long term character shifts that are built on habits you can maintain and the beliefs that undergird them. Establish those over time. Give yourself room to fail but keep moving forward.

FIND YOUR TEAM

I saw a meme today that said, "I never thought the hardest part of being an adult would be making friends." I think they might be right. It's one thing to have people to hang out with and agree about things. It's another thing entirely to find people who are willing to stick with you, hold and be held to a common pursuit, and then disagree when needed. You're lucky to find one such person, and really lucky if you're married to them.

Phase two, the next interior circle inside the target, is to build your team. In a family, it's the most obvious, and also the most difficult. Your team is most likely your spouse, though your parents and in-laws and relatives nearby can certainly be part. Don't downplay your own need for friends who are striving toward healthy, creative purpose like you are. I believe that common purpose and trust are actually more important than family. If you're part of something larger than yourself, a truth worth pursuing, then that truth is far more long-term an investment than even your family.

I say that on the one hand, but I also need to reinforce that the stability of your household is paramount to your children's success. That means your marriage. In fact, improving your marriage is one of the most important things you can do for your kids' long-term happiness. Not only does your healthy relationship give them something to rely on, it gives them a model of how commitment works: through thick and thin.

The research, as I've mentioned previously in this book, about involved fathers in particular is very strong. Your children's mental health is highly influenced by their father's active presence. Rough housing, adventurous risk, and high expectations all come more naturally from the masculine side of the marriage. Of course there are exceptions, but you can't discount the impact of testosterone on personality, regardless of culture.

The team should be built on common purpose and trusting relationships. That means finding people who are in a similar time of life as you, or have at least the same type of commitment to growth in whatever pursuit they've aimed for. Many of these principles of habit and belief are incredibly useful in any leadership role, and that's what parenting is, fundamentally. You are leading your kids toward success in relationships and purpose.

The hard part is that you'll find lots of people who have common interests and are nearby. Proximity and hobbies aren't enough to make a real team. Some people want to watch others lead, or just like to argue about the right way to do things. That's no good either. What you need is to find a church. Now church is a loaded term, to be sure, but I mean something specific when I use it. A church can be a building, or somewhere people listen to lectures and have sing-alongs. Some churches are in homes and based on discussions. Fundamentally, all churches are groups of people aiming at the same set of truths who are willing to help each other get there.

It gets tricky when people come into your life, to your church, who say one thing and do another. That's the danger of all aiming, and it's more severe the higher the aim. There are a lot more fake Navy Seals than there are real ones, but no one is pretending to be the guy who's swabbing the deck. The question is, what do you do with the fakers who want to join your team? It's easy to say that you should cast out the toxic people from your life, but the threat of being alone is real, and an increasing concern in technology-infused communities.

People are lonelier than they've ever been, and the more they report being so, the more likely they are to suffer from chronic and significant health issues. You need people in your life, and if you can't find the highest level of friendship, there's nothing wrong with appreciating what you have. Who's to tell if those friendships won't develop into something more with time and investment.

One last thing about building your team: you need to make sure you're a good teammate if you think people will want to join you on the journey to meeting your potential. We each have areas in which we drop into the power struggle mentality, or times when we are feeling extra insecure and in need of attention. Maybe you have a handle on your mind-set at work, but you know that with your husband or wife things get tense way more often then they should. Maybe home works well, but when you're around your siblings or your parents you fall back into immature patterns. Whatever the setting, know that you can't expect them to be what you need if you're not willing to be there for them. Hold yourself to a high standard, and you'll attract people who do the same. Eventually.

EXPLORE, RISK, CREATE

In exploring the highest level of work, I was trying to put my finger on the word that best expresses it. What is it about the people you know who work at a high level and make it seem effortless? What do they do, how do they think in ways that others don't? I looked at teachers I admire, thought-leaders in a wide variety of fields, and moments of creativity that I had experienced myself.

Adventure was part of it. They were willing to take risks, and they didn't hesitate to try new things. They didn't fear failure and loved seeking innovation, but they didn't throw out the lessons of the past either. In fact, the past practice was critical in seeing things rightly. Fads were never part of what they were doing, even if they became influential in creating them. Trends in every field are usually half the story, a reaction to something that was off balance before. Trendy people create their own pendulums of sorts, as they can't seem to find balance. It's like a driver who is panicked by a car coming too close. Their overreaction sends them head-on into the guard rail.

What's ironic is that the "creative" fields are most likely to be influenced by trends. Fashion, design, and music are full of people seeking to reinvent the genre and themselves in the process. I truly believe these reinventions are ego-based pursuits, fundamentally, and that true trend-setters don't do this. The creative process is selfless and free. That's also, I believe, why artists are so sensitive to the influence of money and fame into their work. To choose fame and fortune, to "sell out," is to sacrifice the gift.

No one says that a carpenter, a scientist, or a teacher is a sellout. Perhaps that's also because no one is clamoring to sign them up for record deals and pay them big money. But carpenters, scientists, and teachers can be artists nonetheless. They can work in a creative way that solves problems and gains insights into the world as it really is. They can take creative risks, and they can find joy in a job well done, regardless of whether anyone notices.

I once sat in on a seminar on how to give teachers effective feedback about their performance. To start the session, they had a debate of sorts, where participants would walk to the place that represented their opinion. On one side of the room there was a paper that said, "Teaching is an art." On the other side, "Teaching is a science." People gravitated to both sides, but the majority of people ended up clustered in the middle.

They think it's both. The more I thought about it, I wanted another place to stand. I think art is science, and science is art.

Most of the science that you've been exposed to, in whatever science classes you've take, you didn't actually do any science. You did something like the history of the discoveries of other people. The people were thinking about and testing ideas within their respective fields of science, but you only got to see those ideas after the fact. That's not science, even if it is really important. The real scientist, like the real artist, is testing and trying different things in search of the truth. When they find it, they somehow also find beauty.

Scientists and artists often get so focused on one way of expressing or understanding what they're exploring that it seems like only a handful of people in the world know what they're talking about. In the process, however, they start to learn about the whole universe. A novel might be the story of one particular character in a proposterously invented universe, but written well, such a novel will show you a picture of your own struggle.

In both science and art, ego is the enemy. Protecting your reputation, worrying about your insecurities, thinking you're better than others, these are all facets of the ego. When you can put down your own question of value and take up the pursuit of balanced and healthy marriage, family, and purpose, you will find that you too are an artist, and you begin to be free.

The bullseye is the hardest to hit. It won't come naturally, and a big part of you will feel the pull toward stopping once you've gotten a team. I want to challenge you to do more, because the bullseye is the best part. The inevitable result of living creative risk, exploring the world to see it as it is, is that people will come to oppose you. Their fear will get in the way, their need for control and safety will make them want to stop you. The closer you get to them, the stronger that urge will feel. Your spouse is the first person you need to bring on your team, but they're also the most likely to fear what you're doing.

Every system of which you are a part, whether it's your family, your community, or your career, will all have in it people who use fear as their motivation, and will think you a fool if you choose to walk away from it. Those people have made for themselves precious circles of control, and if you step into them without paying honor to their particular way of seeing the world, you will be an enemy. If you're going to aim for the center of the target, the highest form of creative freedom, selfless purpose and generosity, then prepare for those people. They will test your resolve and stir up your own fears. Don't fall for it. Train your children not to fall for it either. It will bring healing where others are wounded, and life for generations to come.

Luke Zedwick has known he would be a teacher since he was in fourth grade. He worked in education for 19 years as a teacher or building principal at every level: elementary, middle, and high school. Luke has developed a system to help you understand how we all struggle from an early age. He has been privileged to share his insights in Sierra Leone, Indonesia, and around the US.

Currently, he is training teachers and leaders as a consultant to businesses and school districts, as an Adjunct Professor of Education at Corban University, and as a Missionary to the American Family in churches throughout the Pacific Northwest. He has a passion for leadership that transforms, and he believes that parents are on the frontline of the fight for our future.

You can find him at:

LukeZedwick.com

or on YouTube, Facebook, and Instagram.

Made in the USA
Columbia, SC
07 June 2021